PENGUINS

PENGUINS

Look for these and other books in the
Lucent Endangered Animals and Habitats series:

The Amazon Rain Forest
Antarctica
The Bald Eagle
Bats
The Bear
Bighorn Sheep
Birds of Prey
The Cheetah
Chimpanzees
The Condor
Coral Reefs
The Cougar
The Crocodile
Dolphins and Porpoises
The Elephant
Frogs and Toads
The Galápagos Islands
The Giant Panda
The Jaguar
The Koala
The Leopard
The Manatee
The Orangutan
Owls
The Rhinoceros
Seals and Sea Lions
Snakes
The Tiger
Turtles and Tortoises
The Wetlands
The Whale

PENGUINS

BY KAREN POVEY

Endangered Animals & Habitats

LUCENT BOOKS®

THOMSON
™
GALE

San Diego • Detroit • New York • San Francisco • Cleveland • New Haven, Conn. • Waterville, Maine • London • Munich

On cover: A large colony of King penguins congregates in Antarctica.

LIBRARY OF CONGRESS CATALOGING-IN-PUBLICATION DATA

Povey, Karen, 1962–
  Penguins / by Karen Povey.
    p. cm. — (Endangered animals and habitats)
Summary: Examines the shrinking numbers of penguins due to the pollution of ocean
waters and dangers from humans.
Includes bibliographical references (p.).
  ISBN 1-59018-275-8 (hardback : alk. paper)
  1. Penguins—Juvenile literature. 2. Endangered species—Juvenile literature. 3. Birds,
Protection of—Juvenile literature. [1. Penguins. 2. Endangered species. 3. Birds—
Protection.] I. Title. II. Endangered animals & habitats.
  QL696.S473P69 2003
  598.47—dc21
                             2003000409

Printed in the United States of America

Contents

Introduction

PENGUINS ARE AMONG the most popular and admired of the world's wild animals. Humans feel a strong affinity for these birds whose markings bring to mind a small man wearing a tuxedo. This impression is reinforced by their upright posture, which combined with a clumsy, waddling gait, brings an almost reflexive smile to the face of an observer. Their endearing appearance has earned penguins a prominent place in popular culture and these birds regularly appear in cartoons, children's books, and commercials.

Despite the penguin's star status, its true nature is really not well understood by most people. In reality, penguins rarely live up to their popular image. Penguins are noisy, smelly, and often ill-tempered. Moreover, they spend most of their time not waddling clumsily about on shore, but swimming at sea, far from land. In fact, penguins spend up to 75 percent of their lives at sea, making it difficult to observe even the most fundamental aspects of their behavior. As a consequence, even biologists who have studied penguins for decades admit that much about these birds remains a mystery.

The development of specialized research techniques is beginning to help scientists unravel some of those mysteries. Satellite tracking transmitters and other technological devices are now providing glimpses into the private, seaborne lives of penguins. Gaining this type of knowledge is becoming increasingly important as scientists realize that successful conservation efforts depend on understanding the penguin's interaction with its environment. Such conservation efforts are ever more urgently needed, for despite people's affection toward them, human activities are increasingly putting these creatures at risk of dramatic decline—even extinction.

Human impact on penguin populations is a relatively recent phenomenon. Indeed, penguins were unknown to Europeans until near the end of the fifteenth century. The first reports of penguins were made by explorers sailing off the coast of southern Africa in 1497. Then, in 1520, Ferdinand Magellan and his crew became the first Europeans to see penguins in the New World. A crewman, known to historians only as Pigafetta, kept the records of Magellan's journey, and he recorded his impressions of strange birds he and his fellow adventurers encountered off the coast of South America—creaturers he referred to as geese: "After following the coast towards the Antarctic pole, they came to two islands full of

Although people respond to the penguin's droll appearance, it is actually a smelly and ill-natured creature.

geese and sea wolves [seals and sea lions] in such numbers that in one hour they were able to fill their five ships with geese, and they are completely black and unable to fly and they live on fish, and are so fat that it is necessary to peel them; they do not have feathers and have a beak like a crow."[1]

For centuries after discovering them, Europeans viewed penguins as a resource to be exploited. People collected their eggs, hunted them, and destroyed their nests. These abuses have decreased, thanks to national and international laws to protect penguins. Still, penguins face a number of significant challenges as a result of human activities. Commercial fishing, ocean pollution, oil spills, and global warming all may be playing a considerable role in the reduction of penguin numbers. As the twenty-first century opens, ten of the world's seventeen penguin species are listed on the Red List of Threatened Species compiled by the International Union for Conservation of Nature and Natural Resources (IUCN), a conservation organization that tracks the status of wildlife around the world.

It would seem nearly unimaginable that an animal congregating in such enormous numbers—sometimes in the hundreds of thousands—could be at risk. But biologists worry that once damage to the oceans—where penguins spend most of their lives—reaches a critical point, these large populations could crash with little warning and with little hope of recovery. By raising public awareness of the growing crisis in the world's oceans and taking action now, biologists hope to avoid catastrophe and secure a future for penguins.

1

Meet the Penguins

MOST PEOPLE THINK of penguins as creatures bound to an environment of bitter cold and blowing snow, spending their entire lives trudging across Antarctic ice. This popular image of penguin existence, however, applies to only a few species of penguins. Although many penguins do feed and breed in the waters and on the shores of Antarctica and its surrounding islands, more than half of all penguin species are not found in the Antarctic at all. The majority of penguins live instead in the more temperate regions of coastal South Africa, New Zealand, Australia, and southern South America.

Penguin classification

No matter where they live, all seventeen species of penguins belong to the same family, *Spheniscidae.* These species are grouped into six genera, or subgroups of animals that are most closely related to one another. Penguins in the genus *Pygoscelis* (the Adélie, chinstrap, and gentoo) and the genus *Aptenodytes* (the king and emperor) are perhaps the most familiar because of their classic penguin "look." The members of the *Eudyptes* genus are known as the crested penguins, because clumps of feathers form a plume above the eyes. This genus includes less familiar species such as the rockhopper, macaroni, and erect-crested penguins. The genus *Spheniscus* contains four species of penguins—Magellanic, African, Humboldt, and Galápagos—that are all quite similar to one another but quite different from other penguins. These birds have a more slender appearance as well as

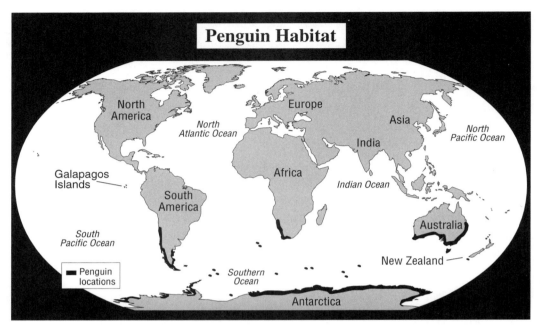

Penguin Habitat

North America

Europe

Asia

North Atlantic Ocean

North Pacific Ocean

India

Galapagos Islands

Africa

Indian Ocean

South America

Australia

South Pacific Ocean

New Zealand

Penguin locations

Southern Ocean

Antarctica

prominent black-and-white banding on their heads and chests. These penguins are primarily fish eaters and live in some of the more temperate regions of the Southern Hemisphere. The last two genera are represented by a single species each. The genus *Eudyptula* describes the little blue, or fairy, penguin of Australia and New Zealand, a small bird with bluish-black plumage on its back. The genus *Megadyptes* describes the yellow-eyed penguin, or hoiho, that nests in solitary burrows in the forests of coastal New Zealand.

What sets penguins apart from most birds is their inability to fly. However, far from being primitive, penguins are considered by scientists to be highly specialized products of long and elaborate evolution. In fact, penguins evolved from flying birds, gradually trading the ability to fly in the air for the ability to swim with a flying motion underwater. Giving up flight provided penguins with the advantage of greatly improved swimming ability that allows them to dive deeply and maneuver quickly underwater while hunting.

Despite their excellent swimming ability, penguins are not found in all the world's oceans. Penguins' distribution depends on two critical factors: the presence of land for breeding, and the presence of cold, nutrient-rich waters for feeding. The frigid currents that emerge from the polar seas are the most productive on Earth, providing a bounty of fish, squid, and crustaceans that form the penguins' food supply. Penguin survival and reproduction is so dependent on these currents that their distribution can be directly linked to ocean temperatures. Penguins are only found where waters are less than 68 degrees Fahrenheit. The one exception to this rule is the Galápagos penguin that inhabits islands along the equator. This species is able to survive in these waters as a result of a cool current flowing from the South American coast, keeping the ocean temperature there at an average of 73 degrees Fahrenheit—much cooler than other waters near the equator.

Interestingly, penguins are never found in the Northern Hemisphere, even though conditions near the North Pole would seem ideal for their needs. The reason is that as penguins evolved and spread through the southern oceans, the warm waters near the equator formed an effective roadblock to their further distribution. Penguins were never able to cross those expanses of warm equatorial waters that produced only limited food for them to eat. Penguins, therefore, never colonized the waters of the Arctic.

Aquatic adaptations

Although humans mostly observe them on land, penguins are considered pelagic—that is, they spend the majority of their lives away from land. In fact, some penguin species are at sea for up to 75 percent of their lives, coming ashore only to breed and incubate their eggs. Penguins are supremely adapted for exploiting the abundant food resources of the Southern Ocean (Antarctic Ocean). Penguins are quick and agile in the water owing to their streamlined, torpedo-shaped, and highly flexible bodies. To enhance streamlining, a penguin's webbed feet are positioned at the very rear of its body where they are used for steering. Although these feet are webbed, they are not used for propulsion; instead, the penguin uses its flipper-like wings to "fly" through the water. In his book *Penguins,*

Penguin Recognition

Penguin bodies are fairly uniform in color and pattern; the main differences in penguin markings can be seen on their heads. William Ashworth explains the significance of these markings in *Penguins, Puffins, and Auks: Their Lives and Behavior:*

One of the main purposes of differences among species—along with helping them fit into their particular ecological niche—is to help members of a given species identify other members of the same species, for breeding, cooperative hunting, child raising, and other species-specific tasks. Markings that have this purpose are called *recognition marks.* In the penguins and auks, they are almost always concentrated in the region of the head. The reason for this is related once again to the set of niches that they fill, and should be clear to anyone who has watched them for very long. As pelagic birds, the penguins and auks spend most of their lives bobbing about on the surface of a broad sheet of water, far from land. They are relatively heavy birds for their size, and they tend to ride low in the water. Under these very common circumstances, the head is the only part of the bird that can be seen easily. So the three pygoscelids [a group of Antarctic penguin species], for example—otherwise almost identical in appearance—have easily distinguishable heads: all black for the Adélies, black with a white band across the top for the gentoos, and white chinned—with a thin black line—for the chinstraps. You can tell them apart at sea as easily as you can on land, and in fact lifting them out of the water doesn't help a bit.

A chinstrap penguin sits on a pebble nest. Its recognition mark, *a black line under its chin, is quite distinctive.*

Puffins, and Auks: Their Lives and Behavior, William Ashworth describes penguin wings and their function:

> The most striking thing about penguins is undoubtedly their wings, which are unlike the wings of any other bird and, indeed, unlike much of anything else in the animal kingdom. They have been compared to the flippers of seals and walruses, and are sometimes called flippers, but the comparison is not fully apt. Seals' flippers have evolved from legs, and they are still used much as legs are, pulling the animal through the water with the sort of scooping motion made by the hands of human swimmers. Penguins' wings are still wings, and they are still used for flight. The difference between them and the wings of other birds is that they are designed to fly through the water.[2]

Penguins' wings are built quite differently from other birds' wings. They are shorter, flatter, and narrower with a more limited range of motion. The long flight feathers that cover other birds' wings are entirely absent, replaced instead by small, stiff, overlapping feathers. This unique wing design allows the penguin to move quickly and efficiently underwater. Thanks to this adaptation, the largest penguins can reach speeds nearing 11 mph and most penguins average 3 to 5 mph underwater.

Of course, penguins must return to the surface to breathe, so many species of penguins periodically leap into the air as they swim, skimming the water's surface before plunging back in, a behavior known as "porpoising." Porpoising is an efficient motion, because it allows a penguin to take a breath of air without losing momentum. (By contrast, a penguin that breathes by swimming to the surface and lifting its head expends much more energy to regain the speed lost in the process.)

Hunting behavior

Penguins primarily use porpoising for covering large distances, often from one feeding area to another, or from their nesting area to a feeding ground at sea. Once there, they dive or swim underwater in pursuit of prey. Most of the penguin's prey is found in the upper water levels, so they do not generally have to dive very deep or for very long. Most feeding dives take penguins to depths of 50 to 60 feet and last less

Energetic penguins porpoise through rough surf. This behavior allows the birds to breathe while maintaining their forward motion.

than a minute. However, many penguins have been observed diving much deeper and for much longer. Chinstrap penguins, for example, are known to dive to depths as great as 230 feet, and gentoo and Adélie penguins have been recorded remaining submerged for up to seven minutes. Emperor penguins are the record holders; the deepest dive recorded for this species is 1,755 feet, and the longest dive is twenty-one minutes. Researchers still do not know why the emperors make these long, deep dives.

During a penguin's hunting dives, a number of adaptations help it locate and capture its prey. For example, a penguin's eyes are specially adapted for seeing underwater. The surface of the eye, or cornea, is flattened in penguins compared to those of land-based birds, resulting in sharper vision underwater. (As a result of this adaptation, the birds are thought to be slightly nearsighted out of the water.) At the same time, penguins have excellent vision in low light, allowing them to hunt in the deep water where little sunlight penetrates.

The penguin's characteristic black-and-white coloration is also a hunting adaptation, providing camouflage as it pursues its prey. As a penguin approaches a school of fish from below, its dark back tends to blend in to the ocean depths. Conversely, as it swims above its prey, the penguin's white belly

Penguin Species

Most scientists recognize the following seventeen species of penguins and their risk categories assigned by the International Union for the Conservation of Nature and Natural Resources (IUCN), an organization that monitors the status of wildlife worldwide.

Genus *Pygoscelis*		IUCN Category
Adélie penguin	*Pygoscelis adéliae*	Lower Risk
Gentoo penguin	*Pygoscelis papua*	Lower Risk
Chinstrap penguin	*Pygoscelis Antarctica*	Lower Risk
Genus *Aptenodytes*		
King penguin	*Aptenodytes patagonica*	Lower Risk
Emperor penguin	*Aptenodytes forsteri*	Lower Risk
Genus *Eudyptes*		
Fiordland crested penguin	*Eudyptes pachyrhynchus*	Vulnerable
Erect-crested penguin	*Eudyptes sclareti*	Endangered
Rockhopper penguin	*Eudyptes chrysocome*	Vulnerable
Macaroni penguin	*Eudyptes chrysolophus*	Near Threatened
Royal penguin	*Eudyptes schlegeli*	Vulnerable
Snares Island penguin	*Eudyptes robustus*	Vulnerable
Genus *Spheniscus*		
Magellanic penguin	*Spheniscus magellanicus*	Lower Risk*
African penguin	*Spheniscus demersus*	Vulnerable
Humboldt penguin	*Spheniscus humboldti*	Vulnerable
Galápagos penguin	*Spheniscus mendiculus*	Endangered
Genus *Eudyptula*		
Little blue penguin	*Eudyptula minor*	Lower Risk
White-flippered penguin**	*Eudyptula m. albosignata*	Endangered
Genus *Megadyptes*		
Yellow-eyed penguin	*Megadyptes antipodes*	Vulnerable

* Some populations near threatened
** A subspecies of little blue penguin

tends to blend in with the light coming down from the sky. This type of camouflage, known as "countershading," likely serves a second purpose as protection for penguins against predators, such as sharks and seals.

Once prey is located, a penguin will catch it with its strong beak, which is specially adapted for that purpose; spiny, toothlike projections on its tongue allow the penguin to grasp a slippery, wriggling fish or shrimp securely. Prey is swallowed whole, often while the penguin is still underwater.

The amount of food a penguin eats per day varies widely with the seasons, with more consumed during the breeding season while the chicks are being raised. One colony of 5 million Adélies was estimated to eat over 17 million pounds of krill and fish each day, or an average of over 3 pounds of food per animal. There is little wonder that a penguin eats so much, since a substantial amount of food is needed simply to keep warm in water that might be as cold as 28 degrees Fahrenheit.

Thermoregulation

Penguins, like all birds, have a high metabolism that results in a body temperature of 100 to 102 degrees Fahrenheit. Helping to maintain that body temperature as the penguin swims is a thick layer of insulating body fat. However, as much as 80 percent of the penguin's insulation is provided by a nearly impenetrable two-layered coat of tightly overlapping feathers. Penguins have more feathers than most other birds, packed as densely as seventy per square inch. The bottom layer of downy feathers traps air close to the penguin's skin to serve as the main form of insulation. The top layer forms a waterproof shield that keeps out moisture and wind. Penguins maintain the waterproofing and insulating ability of their feathers through frequent preening. To preen, a penguin uses its beak to distribute waxy oil over its feathers from the uropygial, or preen, gland near the base of its tail. As it preens, the penguin will realign any feathers that may be out of place in order to keep its plumage in prime condition.

Although the penguin's need to retain warmth is readily apparent, it is just as imperative for penguins to keep cool whenever temperatures rise. The adaptations that allow pen-

guins to live comfortably in cold water may cause them to overheat once they return to land. Antarctic penguins, for example, can develop heat stress if the temperature rises above freezing—32 degrees Fahrenheit.

On land penguins take advantage of special adaptations to achieve thermoregulation. For example, as air temperature rises, blood flow to the penguin's wings and feet increases. In these areas, the blood vessels are located very close to the surface of the penguin's skin. To maximize the dissipation of heat, a penguin will extend its wings, greatly increasing the amount of skin exposed to the air. Penguin species that live in more northerly regions, such as South Africa and the Galápagos Islands, have other adaptations to help them shed heat as

Spreading their wings helps penguins to dissipate heat. If the birds get too warm, they are subject to heat stress.

well. These penguins have bare patches of skin around their eyes and beaks containing high concentrations of blood vessels through which excess heat can radiate. When air temperature is high, blood flow increases dramatically to these areas, cooling the penguin.

In addition to these special adaptations, all penguins can also ruffle their feathers, "unlocking" their weather-tight plumage and thereby exposing their skin to the surrounding air and releasing heat. If temperatures continue to rise, penguins will open their beaks and pant to cool off. They may also bathe in puddles or ponds or retreat, if possible, to the shade of bushes or rock crevices.

Life on land

Beyond keeping cool, penguins face other challenges when they come ashore. For example, the shape and structure of the penguin's body, which serve it so well in the ocean, render it

 Penguin Niches

Although penguins as a group range throughout much of the Southern Hemisphere, each species is limited to a particular distribution. Some species of penguins may have ranges that overlap, but do not compete with one another due to their differing lifestyles. In his book *Penguins, Puffins, and Auks,* author William Ashworth explains:

Each species has its own place in the world, its own well-defined range out of which it rarely wanders; and though the ranges of two or more species may overlap, it will always be found that each type of penguin within the area of overlap pursues a slightly different life-style, so they are never in direct competition with one another. There is a well-known rule of ecology, known as Gause's Principle, which covers this: *two species may not occupy the same niche at the same time. Niche* is used here in the ecologist's sense to mean both a physical space and a role in the dynamics of the environment. Two species cannot occupy the same niche because they would then be in direct competition throughout all aspects of their lives—for nesting sites, for food, even for lookout positions from which to spot and attack the food. The species that was better adapted to their common life-style, even if it was only marginally better adapted, would eventually drive the other species out.

fairly awkward on land. Cherry Kearton, a naturalist who studied penguins in the early 1900s, remarked, "One cannot think of penguins apart from the sea. I imagine that they must regard coming to the island not so much as a holiday, to be enjoyed, as in the light of a painful necessity, to be endured."[3]

What makes movement on land so difficult is the placement of a penguin's feet so far back on its body. This forces the bird to assume an upright posture, severely limiting speed and mobility. The terrain often adds to the penguin's difficulties, although as nature writer Fred Bruemmer notes, some species seem to seek out such challenges. Bruemmer notes that some penguin species, such as the king, Magellanic, and gentoo, tend to make landfall on flat sandy beaches where they can easily come ashore and rest before traveling further inland. Rockhopper penguins, Bruemmer writes, take a different approach, landing on steep, rocky cliffs pounded by powerful waves:

> I first watched these seemingly suicidal landings on the Falklands' small Sea Lion Island, which has a sheer-cliffed east coast exposed to the full power of the subantarctic sea. Great waves roll in from the sea and shatter against the cliff, a mix too frothy for penguin-loving predators such as sea lions. As each wave recedes, a dozen birds cling to the wave-polished rock with strong beaks and long, sharp claws, then struggle upwards with narrow, flailing, hard-edged wings. A few make it up the cliff before the next wave crashes against the birds clinging to the rock and sweeps most of them out to sea. Unfazed, the rockhoppers ride in on another wave, torpedo through the wild water and rush towards the rock wall for another try.[4]

Once on land, penguins use their short, strong legs to walk or hop, often using their beaks for support when the going is especially steep. The rockhoppers described by Bruemmer jump from rock to rock. Larger penguins, such as the emperor and king penguins, are unable to hop, and instead walk slowly, at a maximum speed of 1.7 mph. When snow-covered or icy slopes point in the right direction, these and other species will often lie on their bellies and toboggan over the ice and snow, using their feet for pushing and braking.

Penguin rookeries

The purpose behind the penguins' terrestrial travels is to reach the nesting sites used by their species for countless generations. These breeding grounds are called rookeries, and are used by distinct groups, or colonies, of birds that return to the same area year after year. Breeding seasons vary from species to species; most have an annual breeding season that lasts from spring through summer. Males arrive at the rookery before the females; most return to the same nest site they used the previous year. Females arrive a few days later and select a mate, usually reuniting with the same one from the year before.

Penguins primarily rely on vocalizations, or calls, to recognize one another as they meet at the nest site. These vocalizations, along with physical behaviors called "displays," also serve to establish or reinforce pair bonds. Emperor and king penguins perform one of the most elegant of such courtship displays, described by ornithologist Roger Tory Peterson: "The 'song,' if we may call it that, is delivered by the pair in duet, with heads dipped low against their chests and bills pointed down. In mutual display, they face each other, and after dipping their heads in song, they raise them high while slowly waving their flippers."[5]

Once the pair is established, the penguins will create their nest and breed. Nest sites and materials vary from species to species. Adélie penguins build simple nests of small stones gathered on the ground. Gentoos build nests of small pebbles and feathers. Meanwhile, penguins in more temperate climates, such as Magellanic, Galápagos, and fairy penguins, dig underground burrows for nesting in order to keep eggs and chicks sheltered from the sun. Emperor penguins, however, form colonies on the ice. For this reason, they are not able to build nests at all. Instead, the male balances a single egg on his feet, keeping it warm under a brood, or warming, patch on his belly.

Most penguins, except for emperors and kings, lay a clutch of two eggs, usually four days apart, which incubate from one to two months. The parents will alternate incubation duties with foraging trips to the sea that may last several days. In the case of the emperor penguin, however, the male alone performs incubation duty, warming the egg while the female leaves the breeding area to feed. To stay warm while incubating in temperatures dropping to -75 degrees Fahrenheit and winds gusting to 125 mph, male emperors will huddle together in groups of up to 6,000 individuals.

Regardless of species, when the chicks hatch they are covered by a coat of downy feathers that are not waterproof. As a consequence, chicks are unable to swim; until they grow their adult plumage, they are completely dependent on their parents for food. The parents will take turns at the nest protecting the chicks while the other heads to sea in search of food. The returning adult may be mobbed by many hungry chicks, but regurgitates food only for its own, which it recognizes by their vocalizations. Providing two rapidly growing chicks with sufficient food, however, is nearly impossible. The chick that hatches first usually gets the most food, and in most cases is the only one to survive.

King penguins nest in their rookery, patiently awaiting the birth of their chicks.

Predation by Seals

Leopard seals are well known for preying upon Antarctic penguins. In his article "The Seal's Own Skin Game," published in *Natural History,* author Gordon S. Court recounts his experiences observing seals hunting:

The first leopard seal that I ever saw was in pursuit of an adult Adelie penguin in one of the most spectacular chases I have witnessed. The seal had been floating about 150 yards offshore. When a pod of Adelies was perhaps thirty yards away from the shore, the seal submerged. In a few seconds, swirling eddies arose from below, and the penguins, which had been porpoising out of the water in tight formation, exploded from beneath the surface like fighter jets in starburst formation, each taking a separate heading back out to sea. The seal resurfaced; then with one mighty stroke of its forelimbs, disappeared underwater again.

For long, suspenseful moments, the chase of one Adelie continued underwater; rapid changes in the direction of the bubbles indicated that the seal was in hot pursuit. Suddenly, the zigzag changed to a straight line, an all-out test of speed with both animals rising, arcing, and resubmerging in synchrony. An Adelie penguin on land is an ungainly thing, but in water, it moves like a salmon and, when traveling fast, clears the surface every few seconds to breathe. To see an eleven-foot-long leopard seal, weighing perhaps 800 pounds, match this performance, stroke for stroke, is spectacular. The chase lasted for some minutes, long enough for four scientists working in different parts of the penguin rookery to look out to sea and watch the Adelie successfully outdistance the seal.

At the height of the breeding season, penguin nesting grounds are busy places that may be populated by as many as several hundred thousand or even millions of birds. Penguins are combative creatures and squabble bitterly with one another. They spend a great deal of time calling and displaying to neighboring birds in order to proclaim their territory and defend the nest site. As a result, a penguin chick grows up in deafening, chaotic conditions.

Not only is the penguin rookery noisy, it also is smelly, although how those conditions affect the penguins is uncertain. For humans, however, the first impression of such a place can be unpleasant. James Gorman, author of *The Total Penguin,* provides a vivid description of human sensory effects of a colony of penguins.

On the casual visitor, the calls of penguins have a powerful effect in readjusting one's sense of just what these birds are like. Noise is one of the two overwhelming realities of a penguin colony. When thousands of birds proclaim news of themselves at the same time, the effect is overwhelming. Then, to get the full effect, add the impact on another sense, the other, overwhelming reality of colonial penguin life—the odor of excrement . . . they simply stand in their own accumulating guano. The guano stains of penguin colonies can be seen from the sea long before the birds themselves are visible. Satellites in space can identify large penguin colonies by the pink or white guano patches on dark rock. Anyone with a nose, approaching an island on a ship, can smell a penguin colony from well offshore. [6]

Because penguins are such combative and vocal birds, the noise level in a large rookery is deafening.

The noise and chaos, together with the size of the colony, creates an impression of almost limitless numbers of penguins, as Gorman notes:

> Here are acres and acres of gaping beaks, of birds falling down on the pastel turf, of penguins shouting about things of tremendous importance to them, but a mystery to us. Here are birds in numbers such that they don't seem like birds at all, but more like some kind of cultivated plant crop sprouting up and down the fertilized hillsides—vast rolling fields of penguins.[7]

Because penguins can be found in such enormous numbers and primarily dwell in regions without human populations, it may appear that these birds are safe from the pressures to survive faced by other types of wildlife. This, however, is not the case. Penguins are vulnerable to population declines resulting from a wide variety of human activities. Damage to their environment and direct persecution have been impacting penguins ever since the first Europeans ventured into the southern ocean.

2

Threats to Penguins

DESPITE THEIR LARGE numbers overall, some species of penguins are in danger of becoming extinct. Hunting historically reduced penguin populations, and now competition for food, destruction of rookeries, and contact with humans, however well meaning, are further threatening these birds.

For nearly four centuries after their discovery of penguins in the late fifteenth century, Europeans who traveled to the New World on expeditions that lasted many months or even years fed on these birds. Penguins, which had little or no fear of humans and were unable to fly, proved easy prey. Ships' diaries recorded the numbers taken, often up to three thousand a day and totaling as many as fifty thousand during the voyage of one Dutch ship. Diaries also noted the relish with which a meal of penguin meat was consumed: "Spent forenoon skinning the Emperor—a male, very fat. Half the breast and the liver was a substantial meal for 16 men with nothing else but some peas, cocoa, and biscuit. We fried it in butter and it was excellent."[8]

Commercial exploitation

So plentiful were penguins, however, that even the killing of adult birds by the thousands for food had relatively little impact on their numbers. Far more harmful was the first significant threat that emerged in the 1800s as a result of humans' quest for whales and elephant seals. Crews of hunters roamed the sea capturing these animals for their blubber, which was boiled down to produce oil for use as fuel for lamps. In order to render the blubber, or boil it down into oil, the whalers needed fuel to fire their furnaces. Coal was expensive, and wood scarce on the islands closest to the whaling grounds. But penguins, with their thick layer of fat, could be burned for fuel. As the naturalist Remy Marion noted, whaling crews "fed their furnaces with penguins, throwing them barely unconscious into the fire like logs."[9]

Eventually seal and whale populations declined because of overhunting and hunters, rather than burn the penguins, would render their fatty carcasses for oil. Penguin oil might be used to top off a ship's load of seal or whale oil, or in some cases make up entire ships' cargoes. For example, one notorious penguin rendering operation in the 1800s was located on Macquarie Island, between New Zealand and Antarctica. This island was the nesting site for two enormous colonies of king penguins. For twenty-five years, Marion writes, "royal penguins as well as king penguins were herded like sheep into digesters [boilers], at a rate of 4,000 birds per day or 150,000 per year. They were clubbed at the foot of the furnace and sometimes thrown in alive."[10] Public outcry ended the Mac-

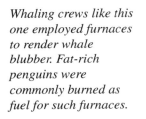

Whaling crews like this one employed furnaces to render whale blubber. Fat-rich penguins were commonly burned as fuel for such furnaces.

quarie Island operation in 1918, but only after royal and king penguins had nearly become extinct there. Penguins were also slaughtered for oil in South Georgia and the Falkland Islands. In the Falklands, nearly five hundred thousand rockhopper and king penguins were killed in just four years. King penguins were especially vulnerable to hunters due to their habit of nesting on open, easily accessible terrain; they were completely exterminated from the Falklands.

Although penguins in more temperate regions were largely spared from this type of large-scale slaughter, they suffered from a different type of commercial activity—the collecting of their eggs by European colonists, who relished them for food. Because penguins nest in great concentrations in a limited number of breeding sites, egg gatherers, with minimum effort, were able to collect enormous numbers of penguin eggs, resulting in almost total breeding failure for some rookeries. For example, on Dassen Island, off the South African coast, egg collection took place on a staggering scale. Between 1900 and 1930, nearly 13 million eggs were taken, with a peak of six hundred thousand taken in 1919 alone. This practice was discontinued in 1967, but it led to huge population declines of African penguins. Today about two hundred thousand birds remain from a population once numbering several million. Elsewhere, egg gathering continues, although on a smaller scale. In the Falkland Islands, residents still gather small numbers of gentoo penguin eggs from nesting areas located near farmland. These eggs used to be an important food source for settlers in the region, but now the practice of collecting gentoo eggs is dying out thanks to the ready availability of chicken eggs. Today egg collecting has virtually no impact on the gentoos' numbers there.

The guano trade

The exploitation of penguins was not limited to the taking of the animals and their eggs, but also extended to the trade in penguin droppings, or guano, which was highly prized as a fertilizer. Because penguins return to the same breeding sites year after year, this guano accumulates around their nests in deposits as thick as 180 feet. The harvesting of guano had no

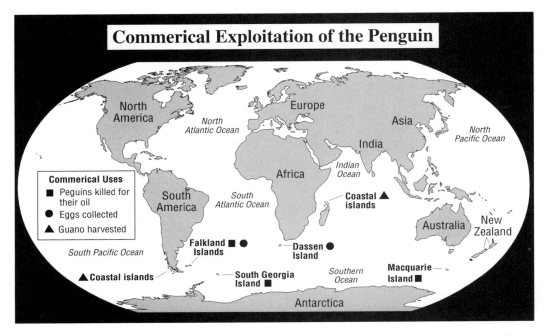

Commerical Exploitation of the Penguin

North America

North Atlantic Ocean

Europe

Asia

North Pacific Ocean

India

Indian Ocean

Africa

Commerical Uses
- ■ Peguins killed for their oil
- ● Eggs collected
- ▲ Guano harvested

South America

South Atlantic Ocean

Coastal ▲ islands

Australia

New Zealand

South Pacific Ocean

Falkland ■ ● Islands

Dassen ● Island

Macquarie Island ■

▲ Coastal islands

South Georgia Island ■

Southern Ocean

Antarctica

direct bearing on adult penguins, but for populations of the *Spheniscus* penguins located on the coastal islands of South America and southern Africa—the Magellanic, Humboldt, and Africa—the effect was devastating, since the birds construct their nests by digging burrows into the guano. With the guano deposits gone, penguin species such as the Humboldt suffered severe nesting failure. As a result, their numbers decreased dramatically.

Human competition

Centuries of penguin persecution have taken their toll and some species have never fully recovered from the harvesting of their oil, eggs, or guano. However, even those species that have yet to see dramatic declines are now under pressure as a result of other human activities. In particular, increased commercial fishing now occurring in the Southern Ocean means that the favored foods of a number of penguin species are in short supply.

Competition between penguins and humans for food is a relatively new phenomenon. Until the middle of the twentieth century, commercial fishing ventures to the waters of the far south, where penguins hunt, were limited; the extreme weather and risks posed by icebergs kept most fishing vessels far to the north. However, as northern fish stocks became depleted, the incentive grew to develop the southern ocean into a fishery as well. Over the later decades of the twentieth century, as the manufacturers of fishing boats developed the technology to deal with the challenges posed by freezing temperatures and floating ice, fishing in the region became big business. Ships from Chile, Japan, Poland, and Ukraine make up the bulk of the current fleet, although recently owners of boats from Australia, Korea, New Zealand, Norway, Russia, South Africa, the United Kingdom, and the United States have either proposed or begun fishing operations in the Southern Ocean as well. The result of intensified fishing in the

Commercial fishing fleets, comprised of boats like these in Tokyo Bay, Japan, harvest huge quantities of fish from the Southern Ocean.

region has been the reduction of some Antarctic fish stocks to as little as 5 percent of their original size. How large the impact of this fishing activity on penguins will be is poorly understood, although scientists speculate that it may eventually play a significant role in reducing penguin numbers by depriving them of the food they need.

Commercial fishing operations are already thought to play a role in the declining populations of the *Spheniscus* penguins, especially the Magellanic, Humboldt, and African. Overfishing in the coastal waters of southern South America and South Africa has left these birds with fewer fish to eat. Between 1956 and 1978, the population of African penguins on the west coast of South Africa plunged by more than half, largely as a result of commercial fishing for anchovy, the penguins' primary prey.

In addition to the competition posed by commercial fishing, penguins face the direct peril of entanglement in fishing nets and lines as they forage. Sometimes penguins are accidentally caught in nets set for fish, an event known as "by catch." The frequency of penguin by catch is unknown, since fishermen who find penguins in their nets are usually reluctant to report such incidents. Penguins are also trapped by nets or pieces of nets that drift in the ocean after being lost or torn. Penguins sometimes become entangled in nylon fishing line that is lost or discarded by recreational fishermen. Any entanglement is usually fatal to penguins, since the nets either prevent the birds from surfacing to breathe or hamper them in their pursuit of prey.

Habitat loss and yellow-eyed penguins

Although fishing activities in their hunting grounds present a threat to most penguins, one species, the yellow-eyed, also suffers due to competition for habitat. Unlike most penguins, which nest in areas that are undesirable for human occupation, the yellow-eyed penguin nests in the forests and shrub lands on the east coast of New Zealand's South Island and smaller nearby surrounding islands—where humans can and do live in large numbers. The nesting areas of the yellow-eyed penguin are facing increasing human pressure as farm-

Krill

Krill is the name generally given to shrimplike crustaceans of the family *Euphausiacea,* but is most often used to describe Antarctic krill, *Euphausia superba.* Antarctic krill is thought to be the most abundant animal species on Earth, numbering as many as 600,000 billion individuals and weighing a total of 650 million tons—heavier than the entire population of the world. Krill mass together in enormous swarms, estimated at weighing 2 million tons and spreading over 270 square miles. These swarms feed on a rich broth of microscopic plantlike organisms called phytoplankton. Female krill lay hundreds of thousands of eggs each year that sink thousands of feet to the bottom of the sea. After hatching, the larvae slowly ascend as they feed, reaching the surface when they are adults at the age of two to three years. During the winter, krill remain under the sea ice where they feed on algae.

These bright red animals, measuring only about an inch in length, form the basis of the entire Antarctic food chain, providing food for baleen whales, seals, fish, penguins, and other marine birds. Virtually every predator on or around the continent either eats krill or krill-eaters. Now humans are joining that food chain by harvesting krill in commercial fishing operations. Krill is largely unappealing to the human palate, however, so most of the catch ends up ground as livestock feed.

ing and logging activities in the region rise. Such activities involve the clearing of land, and without adequate vegetation to provide cover for the chicks, nesting success has decreased dramatically. In addition, cattle and sheep that now graze in the areas favored by the penguins trample nests and eggs. Since the 1960s the yellow-eyed penguin population on New Zealand's South Island has decreased by 75 percent. Although populations on the outlying islands are largely safe from competition with humans and their livestock, today an estimated total of only seven thousand yellow-eyed penguins remain, the second-lowest number of any of the penguin species.

This yellow-eyed penguin is one of only seven thousand remaining of its species.

Introduced predators

An even more serious human-caused problem affecting yellow-eyed penguins and many other species that breed in the more temperate regions north of Antarctica is the introduction of nonnative predators such as rats, cats, dogs, ferrets, weasels, and foxes. These animals arrived with human explorers and colonists and thrived in areas such as New Zealand and Australia where few mammalian predators existed. Penguins evolved in the absence of these types of land-based predators, so are ill equipped to deal with the threats they pose. These predators are able to wreak havoc on the totally defenseless penguins, both chicks and adults.

Introduced predators are an especially severe problem for the little blue penguin of Australia and New Zealand. This is the smallest penguin species, weighing only about two pounds, and is therefore very vulnerable to predator attacks. Weasels, ferrets, and rats raid burrows to steal eggs and kill chicks while domestic cats and dogs attack adult birds. Adults are most vulnerable to dog attacks as they cross the beach and open areas traveling to and from their nest sites. Such attacks can result in significant losses. In one incident in 2001, over the course of two nights wandering dogs killed seventy-two penguins from a single colony in New Zealand, leaving that group with just a hundred breeding pairs.

The impact of tourism

While certain human actions such as fishing and habitat alteration clearly threaten penguins, another human activity once considered harmless may pose a hardship to penguins as well—tourism. Because penguins are generally tolerant of people and nest in large colonies among some of the world's most stunning scenery, they are increasingly becoming a tourist attraction for travelers interested in viewing wildlife. Some penguin viewing opportunities are within easy reach of cities, such as those in New Zealand and southern Argentina. Little blue penguins are a featured tourist attraction in New Zealand where the public may observe the birds parading from the ocean to their burrows at night. At Punta Tombo, in Argentina, a colony of two hundred thousand Magellanic penguins routinely draws tourists. Zoologist Dee Boersma, who studies the birds, compares the sight to a famed wildlife tourist attraction, the wild animals in Africa: "'You can't believe it,' Boersma says of the sight of birds densely packed on the beach. 'It's definitely a spectacle of nature. In my view it rivals things that you see on the Serengeti.'" [11]

Tourism is not limited to penguin rookeries in temperate regions. As modern technology has made polar travel safer and more comfortable for humans, even the farthest reaches of Antarctica are now accessible to sightseers. Antarctic tourism began in the 1960s and remained at low levels until the early 1990s, when tourist numbers began to rise quickly. Passenger numbers grew from forty-eight hundred in the 1990–1991 season to over fourteen thousand in 1999–2000. These numbers are forecast to rise still higher in the future, with predictions of thirty thousand tourists by 2005. Most travelers to the region are expected to arrive eager for close encounters with Antarctic wildlife, especially penguins.

Tourism and Little Blue Penguins

In an effort to raise public awareness about New Zealand's little blue penguins, conservation organizations and public agencies on the South Island joined forces to create a tourist attraction centered on penguin watching. Known as the Oamaru Blue Penguin Colony, this site is an abandoned rock quarry on the edge of town that has been colonized by penguins. Visitors to the colony are able to watch the penguins as they come ashore each night and return to their burrows.

Concerned about the potential negative effects of public viewing on the penguins' behavior, scientists initiated a study to examine the penguins' breeding success. They monitored the growth rates of chicks, finding the Oamaru chicks comparable to chicks in colonies without public viewing. Through eight years of monitoring breeding success, researchers found that chick production at the tourist site was among the highest of all monitored locations for this species. They also found that no breeding adults have moved from the site and almost all chicks remained in the area as well. The great success of this colony may be attributed in part to the active protection it receives against predators, especially compared to other colonies. Since tourism began, the colony has grown from 14 to 105 breeding pairs.

The local community has benefited as well. In 2000–2001 over thirty-two thousand people visited the reserve, all of whom required overnight accommodations. It is estimated that these visitors contributed nearly $3.5 million to the local economy.

A carefully managed program allowing tourists to view little blue penguins (one is pictured here) had no adverse effects on the colony.

Scientists debate what harmful effects, if any, tourism has. Bernard Stonehouse of the Scott Polar Research Institute in Cambridge, England, has studied the impacts of tourism for the last twelve years and reports: "Although there's a lot of apprehension about what tourists might be doing, we found very, very little evidence of anything that's positively detrimental to the environment."[12]

Measuring penguin stress

Other scientists disagree. Dr. Melissa Giese studies Adélie penguin behavior in response to human contact. Giese uses instruments placed inside a dummy egg to measure the penguin's heart rate. Giese observed that penguins approached by people on average experience a 54 percent rise in heart rate. Giese believes this increase in heart rate results in greater energy consumption that could sap an animal's energy reserves while it is incubating, potentially forcing a penguin to abandon its egg and return to the sea for food. In any case, if a penguin is approached too closely, it sometimes leaves its egg, exposing it to freezing temperatures that will kill the unhatched chick unless the parent returns promptly. Giese concludes, "Most people who go [to view wildlife] want to get nice and close to the animals. They [the penguins] can suffer quite dramatic behavioural and physiological reactions to humans. Their incubation behaviour will be interrupted."[13]

Giese is also concerned about the possibility of disease transmission by tourists:

> There is also the potential for the tourists to introduce and spread exotic diseases. If it [such an infection] ever did occur, the effect would be catastrophic. A lot of the tour vessels go to one penguin colony and then three hours later they will be landing at another colony. If they were introducing non-indigenous pathogens, there is a great potential for them to be transporting those from penguin colony to penguin colony.[14]

In addition to their concern for Antarctic wildlife populations being stressed by human visitors, most conservationists have grave concerns that, eventually, a tourist vessel will have an accident that results in a major fuel spill. When tourism in the region began, most of the ships consisted of

In a staged photo, a formally dressed visitor doffs his hat to a colony of penguins. Although the photo is humorous, environmentalists have genuine concerns about human-penguin contact.

converted Russian icebreakers, which were well equipped for travel in the harsh conditions. Today, however, many ships are not specifically designed for polar travel and lack protection from encounters with ice. Today's vessels are also larger, and less maneuverable among the ice floes.

The potential harm from Antarctic tourism has led the Antarctic and Southern Ocean Coalition (ASOC) to voice its strong concerns. In its *Antarctic Tourism Information Paper,* the organization notes, "The fundamental problem with tourism remains not only its potential environmental impacts, but also its effect on Antarctic institutions and on the perception of, and attitudes to, Antarctica as a special wilderness region."[15] In other words, the ASOC believes that the Antarctic should not be a destination for mass tourism not only due to the risks of harm to the environment, but also because tourism by its very nature detracts from the uniquely wild quality of the Antarctic.

In order to prevent what might possibly be irreversible harm to Antarctica and its wildlife, many conservationists are calling for placing greater limitations on and oversight of tourist operations as well as establishing new standards for the design and operation of tourist vessels. How much good increased regulation would do is uncertain. Rules already in place limit the number of people who may land at a given place at a given time to one hundred, and people are asked to keep their distance from penguins. But, notes Giese, not all tour operators enforce the rules: "Some are pretty lousy, allowing people to go close to wildlife, and turning a blind eye to people who collect bits and pieces, artifacts or penguin eggs or whatever." [16]

Even scientists themselves, despite their best intentions, occasionally find their activities negatively impacting Antarctic penguins. Some four thousand people work at Antarctic research stations annually, creating significant amounts of trash and sewage. Garbage has been dumped at sea, burned in open pits, or simply allowed to pile up. At some bases, accumulated trash included leaking fuel drums and other dangerous wastes. At the site of one abandoned research station, biologists discovered Adélie penguin chicks contaminated with oil that likely leaked from discarded fuel drums.

The threats penguins face as a result of direct contact or competition with people and their activities are generally conceded by researchers to be serious. Of greater concern, however, are the devastating consequences confronting penguins through the pollution of their ocean habitat, where these birds spend the greatest proportion of their time.

3

Ocean Pollution

ALTHOUGH MOST PENGUINS make their homes in remote regions, far from human settlements, they are nevertheless increasingly threatened by human activities. Yet even when people are nowhere near, the far-reaching effects of their actions, in the form of pollution, are apparent in the world's oceans—where penguins spend the bulk of their time. Furthermore, once penguins are exposed to marine pollution, treating and rehabilitating affected birds is a difficult and time-consuming process.

Heavy metal contamination

One form of pollution that may affect penguins is the presence in the marine environment of heavy metals, such as lead, cadmium, and mercury. These elements, incorporated into manufactured products themselves or present in industrial waste, show up in even remote areas, carried on the wind or ocean currents. Heavy metals are especially dangerous to predatory wildlife such as penguins because these substances bioaccumulate. That is, they enter the bottom of the food chain in low concentrations in the bodies of organisms such as plankton. Then, because they are not excreted, these metals become increasingly concentrated in organisms further up the food chain. For example, the krill feeding upon plankton will accumulate higher heavy metal concentrations; penguins feeding on the krill will accumulate higher levels still. Although scientists are not yet sure how heavy metals affect penguins, studies of other birds have demonstrated that ingesting these substances can cause infertility, or deformed or unhealthy chicks. In adult birds, when heavy metals reach a high enough concentration, the result is illness and death.

Although studies aimed at measuring levels of heavy metals in penguins are limited, several have taken place. In one project, researchers evaluated the presence of lead in the droppings of penguins deposited over the past three thousand years in a site in Antarctica. They found that the lead concentration significantly increased during the last two hundred years, most notably within the last fifty years. This suggests to Liguang Sun and Zhonqing Xie, the scientists conducting the study, that "global environmental pollution has affected the Antarctic ecological system."[17]

Plastic pollution

Another form of pollution known to affect penguins, although to an unknown degree, is the presence of plastic debris in the oceans. It is estimated that nearly half a million

Metal pollution affects the marine food chain. Metal accumulates in plankton, which are eaten by krill (pictured), which are in turn consumed by penguins.

plastic containers and objects find their way into the ocean every day. These plastics and other trash, tossed overboard by crews on recreational and commercial vessels alike, now foul all the oceans and the shores of even Earth's most isolated landmasses.

Plastic is not subject to decomposition, as is organic matter such as paper and wood. As a result, these items made from plastic will remain in the environment as hazards for wildlife for extremely long periods of time. Although just how many penguins are harmed by this plastic trash is uncertain, the harm to individual animals has been well documented. Some items, such as the rings that hold six-packs together, trash bags, and strapping material can entangle penguins, preventing them from hunting effectively or escaping from predators.

The greatest danger from plastic trash, however, likely results from ingesting smaller bits, created when waves break up larger plastic items such as food containers or fishing floats. Penguins consume these plastic bits directly, mistaking them for food, or consume fish that have themselves swallowed the pieces. This plastic is not digestible, nor does it move through the digestive tract. Instead, it remains inside the penguin. Eventually, penguins can wind up carrying large amounts of plastic pieces in their digestive tracts. Adult birds can regurgitate some of this plastic, but since regurgitation only happens in the process of feeding the young, the plastic ends up in chicks' stomach instead. In extreme cases, some chicks may end up starving to death because their stomachs are full of plastic, leaving no room for food.

Oil pollution

Far more clearly documented than the effects of plastics and heavy metals on penguins is the impact of oil pollution. Oil enters the ocean from a variety of sources including shipwrecks, discharge from tankers and freighters, and runoff from land. This daily discharge of oil into the sea is proving to have devastating consequences for penguins.

Oil harms penguins in a number of ways, but the greatest numbers of birds are harmed when they come in direct contact with oil in the form of a slick, the pool of oil that forms on

Oil Pollution in Antarctica

While the most well-known oil tanker disasters have affected South African penguins, even birds living in the isolation of Antarctica are increasingly facing the same threat, as William Ashworth explains in his book *Penguins, Puffins, and Auks:*

> Economic development and—perhaps to a surprising degree—tourist promotions are extending these threats to the Adélie and emperor penguin populations of the Antarctic. In January 1989, the Argentine cruise ship *Bahia Paraiso* ran aground off Antarctica's Palmer Peninsula, spilling some 170,000 gallons of fuel oil; this was just the most widely publicized of a number of similar incidents occurring in this area before and since, including the grounding of the Peruvian research ship *Humboldt* . . . and the accidental release of more than 50,000 gallons of oil from a U.S. supply bunker onto the ice at McMurdo Sound. The very fact that these incidents are being reported, however, gives us some reason for hope. If no one cared about the lives of these birds, there would be no reason to report their deaths. Caring, we can perhaps do something.

the surface of the water following a spill. When a penguin comes in contact with the oil, its feathers absorb it, which destroys their ability to trap air. As a consequence, an oil-coated penguin will quickly lose its body heat and die of hypothermia, or extreme chilling. Even if the animal gets back to shore before it freezes to death, it will ingest the highly toxic oil in its efforts to clean itself.

As harmful as oil is known to be to penguins, little is being done to prevent such pollution, according to penguin researcher Dee Boersma, who states: "In Argentina, dumping oil offshore is just a misdemeanor with a small fine. For a tanker operator, that's the price of doing business. Besides, the law really isn't being enforced."[18]

The colony of Magellanic penguins Boersma studies at Punta Tombo, Argentina, has suffered a 20 percent decline between 1987 and 1985—a decline Boersma attributes to tankers' dumping of oil-contaminated ballast water off the coast. Based on counts of oiled penguins found dead on the beach, Boersma estimates that 20,000 adult penguins and 22,000 juveniles die from encounters with oil along the 1,800-mile coast of Argentina each year, making oil pollution the main cause of adult penguin mortality in the area.

Oil spills

Although frequent discharges of small amounts of oil may be most dangerous for penguins in general, large-scale oil spills that result from tanker wrecks and other accidents can dramatically affect individual penguin colonies located near the site of the spill. Moreover, many oil spills have occurred in parts of the world inhabited by penguins.

The oil tanker Jessica *lists precariously. Running aground in the Galápagos Islands in 2001, the tanker spilled almost two hundred thousand gallons of oil.*

When a large spill does occur, often there is little to be done, except hope that winds and currents will carry the oil away from areas frequented by penguins. For example, in January 2001 when the tanker *Jessica* ran aground in the Galápagos Islands and spilled nearly two hundred thousand gallons of fuel, nature lovers worldwide worried that the spill

would be catastrophic for the unique ecosystem of the islands. The Galápagos Islands, a World Heritage Site, is one of the most pristine island environments in the world, home to many species of rare wildlife, including the endangered Galápagos penguin.

Fortunately a number of factors combined to lessen the impact of the spill and allow the wildlife of the Galápagos to escape mostly unharmed. The currents and the wind helped move oil away from the islands and the heat of the equatorial sun on the ocean's surface speeded evaporation of the fuel. A quick response by the Ecuadorian navy, the U.S. Coast Guard, and local volunteers in making an effort to contain the spill prevented oil from coming onto shore. As a result, only a few dozen animals—no penguins among them—required treatment. Still, some researchers are concerned about long-term problems and will continue to study the wildlife of the area for evidence of ill effects that may be subtle or take time to discern.

South African oil spills

As tragic as a major spill in the Galápagos might be, it is the penguins living near busy shipping lands that are most affected by such accidents. For example, the penguins of southern Africa have endured repeated spills since 1948, when a spill killed one-third of the colony of African penguins on Dyer Island. The frequency of oil spills in the region increased significantly when military conflict in the Middle East forced the closure of the Suez Canal from 1967 to 1975. During this time, oil tankers traveling between the Persian Gulf and Europe—as many as 650 each month—were forced to travel around the southern tip of Africa. Most of these ships had not been built to withstand the severe weather they encountered in the open ocean and many ran into trouble as a result. For example, in 1968 the *Esso Essen* ran aground in a storm and spilled four thousand tons of oil. An estimated seventeen hundred penguins were oiled and virtually all died despite people's efforts to save them. In the twenty years following the *Esso Essen* accident, six other spills oiled over ten thousand penguins.

Sources of Marine Oil Pollution

Much of the oil encountered by penguins enters the marine environment not as one might imagine—by shipwrecks and the resulting oil spills—but in a much more subtle fashion. In fact, according to a 1990 U.S. Academy of Sciences estimate, fully 37 percent of oil pollution in the ocean enters the sea from land. This pollution is the result of oil-tainted storm runoff from roads and industrial and household dumping of oil products into storm drains. Storm drains carrying this toxic runoff ultimately empty into rivers or the sea itself, carrying a steady supply of oil to oceans annually. One study conducted in Australia, for example, estimated that as much as twenty thousand tons of oil runoff is washed into that country's coastal waters each year.

Despite the impact of this land-based oil pollution, the largest single contributor to oil in the ocean is the shipping industry. The U.S. Academy of Sciences estimates that 45 percent of marine oil pollution comes from shipping, but only 12.5 percent of that is from oil tanker accidents. The majority comes from accidental and intentional discharge of oil into the water.

Thousands of small oil spills take place annually as a consequence of normal shipping activities in seas worldwide. Many of these incidents are accidental. Fuel may spill while a ship is being loaded or a traveling ship's leaking engine may leave a trail of oil behind. Many spills, instead of being accidents, however, are more deliberate. The most common intentional discharge of oil at sea is the dumping of ballast water. Oil tankers take on ballast water to fill their empty tanks after a load of oil has been delivered. This water provides stability for the ship as it returns to collect another load. International law requires that this oily water be pumped out at the terminal once the ship arrives to reload, but this rule is frequently ignored. Crews often discharge the ballast water into the sea shortly before coming into port in an effort to save time before reloading. There is virtually no enforcement of the laws against this practice that results in the dumping of many millions of gallons of oil into the ocean every year.

The havoc caused by the *Esso Essen* wreck was the catalyst for the formation of an organization that would develop techniques and facilities for cleaning oiled seabirds, especially penguins. The goal was to be better prepared to deal with the aftermath of future oil spills. Known as the South African National Foundation for the Conservation of Coastal Birds, or SANCCOB, this group has been responsible for rescuing and rehabilitating tens of thousands of penguins since its founding in 1968.

SANCCOB's techniques were put to the test when the ship *Apollo Sea* sank near Dassen Island spilling twenty-four hundred tons of fuel oil and oiling ten thousand African penguins—representing 5 percent of the world population of this species—in June 1994. This event illustrated the extreme risk oil spills pose to penguins, for despite the efforts of rescuers, 50 percent of the affected birds died from shock or from the oil's toxic effects while being transported to the care facilities or shortly after arriving. The remaining five thousand penguins were cleaned and eventually released.

SANCCOB research shows that the survival rates of penguins that have been oiled, cleaned, and released are virtually the same as those penguins that did not require rescue. Over four thousand of these penguins had identification bands placed on their flippers before their release, allowing researchers to monitor the rehabilitated birds to learn how they fared in the future. Over the following five years, 73 percent

Rescue workers scrub clean an oiled penguin. Suprisingly, the survival rate of such rescued birds is very high.

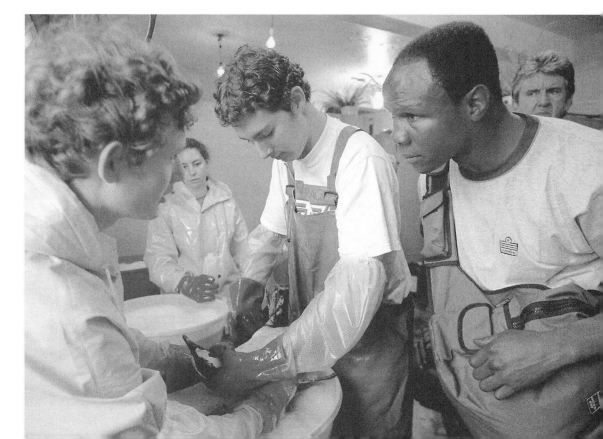

of the banded penguins were seen back at breeding colonies at least once, and 39 percent were known to have bred or attempted breeding. Without human intervention, it is certain that the majority of oiled penguins would have died.

The *Treasure* oil spill

The positive outcome for the penguins that were rehabilitated after the *Apollo Sea* spill was a strong endorsement for SANCCOB's procedures for handling large numbers of oiled birds. However, the death of such a great proportion of birds during transport and the early stages of treatment demonstrated a need for improvement in those areas. Six years later, rescuers had a tragic opportunity to test their new procedures when, once again, disaster struck off western South Africa.

On June 23, 2000, the iron ore carrier *Treasure* sank, spilling thirteen hundred tons of its fuel oil into the water between Dassen Island, which supports the world's largest colony of African penguins, and Robben Island, home to the third largest colony. This spill had the potential to threaten a far greater number of penguins than occurred as a result of the *Apollo Sea* wreck. In this instance, not only were penguins at sea contaminated, but because the spill took place close to shore, penguins at land were also at risk. As oil floated onto the islands, it became clear that this was to become a wildlife disaster of immense proportion. "It is looking at this stage like it will far outweigh the Apollo disaster,"[19] said Christina Pretorius, a spokesperson for one of the groups participating in the rescue effort.

By the next day, oiled penguins began to come ashore on both islands—two hundred to three hundred the first day. In an attempt to keep oil from reaching the area of Robben Island's coast most frequently used by penguins, a floating boom was deployed that would prevent further movement of the oil. However, the boom broke apart that night, allowing oil to come ashore. As a result, all penguins arriving on or leaving the island would come in contact with the oil. The oil had also spread to cover large areas within the penguins' feeding grounds. Within a few days, the oil had also spread to Dassen Island, reaching its shores by June 28.

The timing of this spill, at the height of the breeding season, greatly increased its potential impact. Both islands had large numbers of chicks still in the nest, dependent on their parents: approximately nine thousand at Dassen Island and about six thousand at Robben Island. A census of the islands' penguins had been completed just months before the accident, resulting in an adult population estimate of fifty-five thousand birds on Dassen Island and eighteen thousand adults on Robben Island. Together, the birds on these islands represented 40 percent of the entire African penguin population.

As more oiled penguins continued to make landfall—over three thousand by June 26—rescuers developed a dual strategy for dealing with the disaster. First, oiled birds were to be caught and treated as rapidly as possible to minimize deaths. Second, and just as urgent, was the need to prevent clean birds from becoming contaminated. On Robben Island, both oiled and clean penguins on shore were herded into pens, collected, and transported to one of SANCCOB's holding stations. At the same time, volunteers attempted to clean the penguin landing areas of oil by applying absorbent material

Rescuers work with large numbers of oil-soaked penguins on Robben Island following the Treasure *oil spill of 2000.*

Impressions of a SANCCOB Volunteer

Through postings on the University of Cape Town website, Mike Ford, a volunteer for the *Treasure* oil spill penguin rescue effort describes the challenges of his duties feeding and medicating oiled penguins prior to cleaning at the SANCCOB Salt River treatment center:

> If you don't get the birds under control pretty fast, they seem to nail you on the same spots over and over, so in about an hour and a half—and more for reasons of self-preservation than any other—one becomes an "instant expert" at catching and holding these wriggly little varmints. Once over the initial mastering of the techniques required, one can concentrate on improving so as to cause the birds the least amount of stress in the process. By 1030 [I] was allocated to a feeding team of three feeders and one carrier. This involves entering a designated pen containing about 150 penguins and—sitting on an upturned milk crate and with a bucket of sardines alongside—proceeding to catch one and immobilize it by means of holding it no-so-gently between the thighs and force feeding three sardines plus one special fish containing medication. This process is repeated and repeated. . . .

> I was absolutely amazed and impressed by the team spirit, work and dedication of everyone there, and also by the unbelievable spectrum of different people throwing in whatever time they can spare. . . . The heartbreaking element is, of course, that for every 500 sent out clean, 1,000 new arrivals appear. Nevertheless, there is a light at the end of the tunnel, and that is the light of the will to overcome of all those wonderful people involved.

to the rocks and sand and removing contaminated vegetation. On Dassen Island, priority was given to preventing unoiled penguins from leaving for sea. Groups of clean penguins were contained by fences, then later collected and evacuated. Once all clean penguins were contained, the effort shifted to collecting the island's oiled birds and removing oil from the beaches.

As this penguin rescue effort demonstrates, the effects of an oil spill on colonies of nesting birds poses diverse and serious challenges. For in addition to the many thousands of birds that were oiled immediately, many others were in harm's way. Evacuating the huge numbers of penguins that escaped the oil initially but would become oiled without intervention—nearly twenty thousand birds—was extremely challenging. Resources were already being stretched by the effort to clean oiled birds, and it would have been impossible to care for this many penguins, had they been kept captive. Instead, rescuers decided to relocate the birds to Cape Recife, a coastal area nearly five hundred miles east of the spill. Cape Recife is an important foraging area for a nearby colony of penguins so those overseeing the relocation knew the birds would have sufficient food available upon release. Cape Recife was far enough from Robben and Dassen islands that it would take penguins ten to twenty days to return, ample time to complete the cleanup of the remaining oil.

Cleaning oiled penguins

While clean birds were being relocated, oiled birds were being cared for at several SANCCOB treatment facilities. Rehabilitating oiled penguins, in this case more than nineteen thousand birds, was a painstaking process, possible only with the assistance of hundreds of volunteers, from zookeepers and vets to untrained volunteers. Birds arriving at the center were highly stressed, first from the oiling and then by their capture, so the first step in their treatment was to stabilize them. The penguins were force-fed fluids, to rehydrate them, and activated charcoal to bind with the oil they had ingested, to keep it from entering their bloodstream. In order to increase the penguins' strength for the traumatic experience of being cleaned, volunteers also force-fed them fish.

Cleaning each penguin required two people and took from fifteen to forty-five minutes, depending on the condition of the bird. Each penguin was first pretreated by being coated in vegetable oil, which helped lift the fuel oil from the feathers. After twenty minutes, the penguin was placed in a wash basin filled with warm, soapy water and the team began rubbing the oil off. The vigorous kicking and struggling of the penguin actually aided the process. This procedure was repeated using fresh basins of water until the penguin was clean from the neck down.

The next step was cleansing the penguin's face, its most sensitive area. Using a toothbrush, the washer gently scrubbed around the bird's nose and eyes, rinsing repeatedly. After the

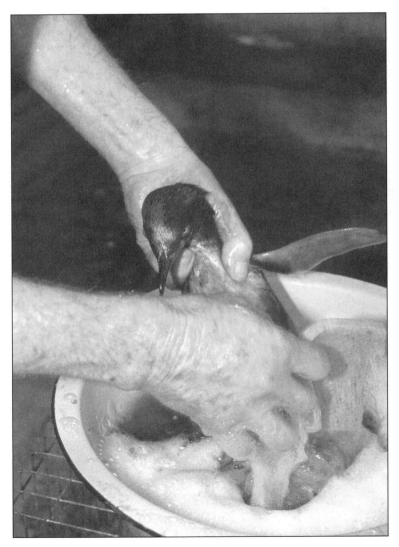

An oiled penguin is washed repeatedly in basins of warm, soapy water.

washer completed a penguin, it was carried to the rinsing station where the soap was sprayed off, then on to the drying station. After cleaning, the penguins were returned to holding pens where they spent approximately a week gaining further strength and restoring the waterproofing on their feathers. Once the birds were fit, they were transported in boxes to the beach and released.

In addition to adult birds treated and released, the rescue team also had to deal with the thousands of chicks orphaned or separated from their parents. Over thirty-three hundred chicks were collected from the nesting areas and sent to facilities to be hand-reared. Of these chicks, nearly three thousand survived to be released.

The rescue outcome

Amazingly, 90 percent of the oiled birds captured for cleaning survived to be released. All told, the mortality of African penguins as a direct result of the spill was about 2,000 adult and immature birds and 4,350 chicks, an incredibly low number in light of the great number of penguins affected. Penguins that were released returned quickly to their home islands, often within a month.

Because it is uncertain what the long-term effects are for penguins that have been oiled and treated, the penguin populations of Dassen and Robben Islands will be monitored for many years to come. Scientists expect that because penguins tend to be monogamous, breeding success may decrease until the many birds that lost their mates form new pair bonds. Scientists also expect that the growth rate of the colony will be reduced due to the death of so many chicks. Still, there is reason to hope for the future of the penguins. In 2001 about three thousand penguins affected by the spill were observed on Robben Island, many of which successfully raised chicks. The penguins of South Africa, despite enduring centuries of harm as a result of human persecution or human activities, continue to survive.

Most scientists agree that pollution of the penguins' ocean environment poses some of the most serious threats to their long-term survival, especially in temperate regions, where pollution is greatest. However, the extent to which pollution and other human-related threats impact penguins is still largely unknown. By studying penguins, especially during their time at sea, scientists hope to gain a better understanding of these birds and their place in the marine ecosystem.

4

Studying Penguins

IN ORDER TO DEVELOP appropriate strategies for protecting penguins and penguin habitat, it is essential that scientists gain a comprehensive understanding of the biology and
behavior of each species. The study of penguins, however,
provides some unique challenges to researchers. Most notable
is the fact that penguins spend the majority of their lives at
sea, an environment that by its very nature is inhospitable to
humans. Most of the information gained from penguin studies
over the last one hundred years relates instead to their lives on
land, especially concerning their breeding and rearing of
young.

Historic penguin studies

The early pioneers of penguin research were the naturalists accompanying the polar expeditions of the early 1900s.
One of the first of these was G. Murray Levick, a naturalist
with Robert Scott's 1910 to 1912 expedition and who studied
Adélie penguins in Antarctica. Scott and eleven others died
on the expedition, but Levick survived, and his accounts of
his work were important because they provided some of the
first insights into penguin biology and behavior. During this
time period, most expedition naturalists viewed the collection of penguins as specimens for museums as their primary
objective and made only cursory notes on their observations
of penguin ecology. In 1936 Robert Cushman Murphy compiled the records of these collectors along with the results of
his own studies to publish *Oceanic Birds of South America.*
This was the most complete account of penguin ecology at

Explorer Robert Scott's ship sets sail on a 1910 Antarctic expedition. Naturalist G. Murray Levick traveled with Scott in order to study Adélie penguins.

the time, and would remain a respected reference for many decades.

Coinciding with the publication of *Oceanic Birds* was the inception of the first in-depth study of penguins, undertaken by an amateur naturalist named Lancelot Richdale. Richdale's study of the ecology of the yellow-eyed penguin in New Zealand was groundbreaking because it was the first to examine a penguin population over the long-term. By placing bands on the penguins' feet, Richdale was able to identify individual birds, record the family relationships between them, and therefore study the population over many generations. He published numerous articles on penguins that did a great deal to popularize the species with the general public. In 1957 he published the scientific account of his study.

Throughout the 1950s and 1960s, study of the polar penguin species advanced greatly as various nations began developing bases in Antarctica, affording researchers more facilities from which they could conduct in-depth research. French, British, New Zealand, and Australian biologists conducted studies and published reports on a wide variety of penguin topics including taxonomy, evolution, anatomy, breeding, behavior, and mortality. Despite the huge advancement in penguin studies during this time period, relatively little attention was given to the nonpolar species; only the Magellanic and little blue penguin were studied in any depth.

Solving a penguin mystery

Gradually many questions regarding penguins yielded to researchers' efforts. One such question that had long baffled scientists was African penguins' laying of two eggs, three days apart. This lag time between eggs means that one chick hatches before the other. As a result, the first chick to hatch will be larger and stronger than the second, and able to compete more strongly for food when the parents return to the nest. Often, if food is in short supply, the younger chick will die without ever leaving the nest.

In a study designed to solve this mystery, two researchers, Yolanda van Heezik and Philip Seddon, investigated this breeding strategy, which at first glance appears not to be in the penguins' best interests. To do this, the researchers moved a number of hatchlings from nest to nest, creating pairs of chicks that were the same age and size. Because adult penguins do not form a permanent bond with their chicks until the youngsters are about two weeks old, the researchers were able to avoid the potential problem of parents refusing to care for the introduced chicks. Over the next four months van Heezik and Seddon monitored two hundred nests: those with the pairs they created of same-sized chicks and control pairs of unequal-sized chicks. They checked the nests daily and weighed the chicks every five days.

The researchers described the challenging task of nest checking:

> Nest checks could be an arduous affair, as most of the penguins, on noting our approach, dived either directly into existing burrows in the soil or into hollow niches under boulders. In areas of sandy soil and guano—prime turf where penguins were packed

together—we had to tread carefully among burrows to avoid breaking through the roofs and exposing the nests to the elements. Some chicks camped deep within rock piles and could be caught only by our lying full length in the mud and guano and jamming one shoulder against the entrance to afford us the longest possible reach. After heavy rain, this was a particularly unsavory chore, made worse by the soggy remains of old chick corpses. While the chicks were young, we had to run the gantlet of parents defending the nest with bill and flippers. The razor-sharp edges and hooked upper mandibles of the beaks were formidable weapons that frequently drew blood and left permanent scars.[20]

By weighing the chicks and observing them being fed by the parents, van Heezik and Seddon believe they found the answer to why it was an advantage for African penguins to have chicks of unequal size. They observed that, as expected, in nests containing different-sized chicks, the chicks that hatched first were able to dominate at feeding time, eat more, and become heavier than their siblings. Eventually, the older chick would leave the nest and begin to forage independently. In years when food was plentiful, the smaller sibling left behind was then able to eat more after the larger chick left, grow quickly and soon become independent as well. However, in nests where the chicks were the same size, neither chick was able to dominate at mealtime. These constantly competing chicks grew more slowly and eventually emerged from the nest at lower body weights than the chicks of unequal sized groups. Although they were both able to survive until fledging, these lower weight chicks, as compared to fat, healthy chicks, had a decreased chance of surviving their first few months at sea as they learned to hunt.

Van Heezik and Seddon noted that this strategy benefits the penguin parents as well:

> The breeding strategy . . . seemingly a biological puzzle that creates competition between siblings and often results in the death of one of them—is ultimately practical and efficient. . . . If one or both chicks go to sea with a healthy and timely start, parent penguins also enjoy an advantage, not having to work so hard for quite as long. Then they too can leave Dassen Island and return to the sea and its many challenges.[21]

Counting Penguins

Census taking, when it comes to penguins, is anything but straightforward. Even though researchers can be confident that they are seeing the same individuals year after year, arriving at a count that is reasonably accurate in the first place is challenging. Penguin counters utilize a handheld counting device known as a tally-whacker. By depressing a knob on the tally-whacker, the census-taker records each bird seen. However, when faced with counting birds on a single plot of land covered with thousands, tens of thousands—maybe even a hundred thousand—penguins, researchers find that because all the birds look so much alike, it is next to impossible to be certain the same bird is not being counted twice. To assure themselves that their count is reasonably accurate, census-takers repeat the count until they arrive at three totals that are within 10 percent of one another.

Counting penguins

Van Heezik and Seddon's research illustrates the use of a time-honored tool in researching animal behavior, direct observation. Another important tool employed by penguin researchers is a census, or a count of individual numbers of penguins in a given area. Counts of penguins are meaningful because individuals of many penguin species return year after year to reproduce in the rookeries where they were hatched. Researchers can be reasonably certain, therefore, that by comparing numbers at each rookery from year to year, they can detect if populations are increasing or decreasing.

Researchers sometimes resort to counting nests, rather than the birds themselves. This strategy enables a census-taker to count large numbers relatively quickly. Ron Naveen, a researcher who has been studying and counting penguins in Antarctica for sixteen years, experienced one day when, in a nine-hour counting session, he tallied a half million penguin nests, representing one million adult birds. Naveen, like other researchers, uses a handheld counting device called a tally-whacker. Naveen describes some of the techniques he uses to ensure accuracy when counting the birds themselves:

I keep my field notebook raised over my left eye and count by moving counterclockwise around the group or colony in question. The penguins to my right are ones I've already tallied. I try to line them up in rows, spying them with my right eye, and count either from top to bottom or bottom to top. . . . You also need to have a decent vantage point, usually high enough so you can see all the penguins in the group you're counting. It would be ideal if you could walk the perimeter of the group, see all the animals at all times, and proceed slowly from one starting point to another. Sometimes a rock in the center or on one edge of a colony will be a convenient marker noting your starting point. Sometimes I've pounded stakes next to rocks or into the ground to assist the orientation. You can't efficiently tally-whack an assemblage of nests or chicks that's greater than a few hundred strong, or perhaps complicated by uneven terrain and a lack of vantage points. If you confront thousands densely massed together, you must resort to approximations—by counting fistfuls or fingerfuls of penguins, with each fistful or fingerful of penguins containing an estimated number of nests or animals.[22]

Counting penguins in colonies as large as this one is challenging. Researchers have developed ingenious methods for census taking.

The Penguin Bible

In his book *Waiting to Fly: My Escapades with the Penguins of Antartica,* penguin researcher Ron Naveen describes the importance of the reference work *The Distribution and Abundance of Antarctic and Subantarctic Penguins,* known in scientific circles as The Penguin Bible. This volume catalogs the sites where Adélie, gentoo, chinstrap, macaroni, and emperor penguins have been recorded breeding as well as the numbers of individuals at each site. Naveen considers this work a major research tool because "ultimately, penguin counts tell us a story. New censuses and data may be compared to old, changes may be detected, and then the question of pinpointing the cause of any such changes can be tackled. New sites, new censuses—all of it adds to the knowledge base."

Different designations are given to the various types of censuses that are conducted. Naveen says,

> My favorite designation in *The Penguin Bible*—[is] a simple letter B. This means 'no estimate of numbers was available. In these cases a colony or colonies are known to exist at that locality, but no further data are available.' Occasionally, a remark suggests that the unsurveyed site is a large colony. The point, though, is that these unknown areas make penguin-counters salivate: They are a chance to add to our overall knowledge of where these animals are located and how many of them exist at a particular location. The more information added to the database, the more we'll be able to understand, over time, whether fluctuations are occurring.

These on-the-ground counts are being increasingly supplemented by counts of birds shown in aerial photographs taken from helicopters. An even more high-tech method—remote detection and counts by satellite—is on the horizon. Currently, satellites can detect large penguin colonies, measuring at least a few hundred yards across. As technology improves, satellites will be able to detect smaller concentrations and send pictures to researchers in their labs, allowing them to count individual penguins without having to enter the birds' actual habitat.

Studying penguins at sea

Scientists have embraced the development of other new technologies that now make it possible to study penguins where they spend the majority of their lives—at sea. A variety of technologies and techniques have significantly advanced penguin research, allowing scientists to follow penguins into the oceans in order to study their swimming, diving, and feeding behaviors, that, until recently, were virtually unknown.

Once such tool is satellite telemetry, used to track the movements of penguins once they leave the land. Penguins to be tracked are captured and fitted with a small, lightweight transmitter. The transmitter, glued to the feathers on the bird's lower back, is encased in a waterproof housing and trails an antenna. The transmitter unit is streamlined and placed as low as possible on the bird's back to minimize any drag, or slowing, the device may cause as the penguin swims. Transmitters used with penguins are generally equipped with a special switch that turns the unit off while the penguin is underwater, therefore saving power and prolonging the life of the transmitter's battery. The transmitter is specially programmed to send the penguin's location to the receiving satellite at specified intervals, such as every forty-five or sixty seconds, when the penguin is on the surface of the water. In addition, some transmitters may also record and send data regarding the frequency of dives, providing information on feeding activity. The researcher can then download the information from the satellite; information on the penguin's movements and whereabouts is generally accurate to within one hundred meters.

Information on a penguin's location is useful for determining the patterns of its movements as well as understanding what parts of the ocean are utilized as penguin habitat. For example, one satellite telemetry study of four king penguins on South Georgia Island showed that the birds swam 240 miles to the north to feed and in a single foraging trip lasting three weeks covered well over 900 miles. In another study of migrating Magellanic penguins in Argentina, telemetry data showed that the birds traveled nearly 500 miles in three

weeks. In this study it was observed that the penguins' migration route was relatively close to shore (within 180 miles), well within the coastal shipping lanes used by oil tankers in the region.

In addition to satellite telemetry transmitters, penguins have also been fitted with a variety of other devices as researchers attempt to measure the remarkable swimming and diving prowess of these birds. For example, several types of speed gauges have been attached to penguins through the use of harnesses and clamps. Similarly attached dive recorders and depth gauges provide data on penguins' diving abilities.

The transmitter attached to the emperor penguin at right is used in satellite telemetry. Such devices track the movements of penguins in the sea.

Does research disturb penguins?

With the increasing use of instrumentation attached to the bodies of penguins, some scientists have begun to examine what, if any, influence this means of gathering data has on the birds' behavior. The results from a variety of studies seem to indicate that there may be an impact. It has been reported that penguins outfitted with transmitters demonstrate significantly reduced swimming speeds, decreased frequency of dives, unusual amounts of pecking or preening, increased use of energy, and decreased nesting success. In addition, some birds carrying transmitters made longer foraging trips; some even failed to return to shore after feeding. However, as technology advances, the equipment employed in research is becoming smaller and less obtrusive. A study reported in 2001 demonstrated that utilizing smaller devices made no differences in the length of Adélie penguin foraging trips between groups of birds with the devices and those without.

Some researchers also worry that the practice of flipper banding, which is used to help observers identify individual penguins, may hamper the penguins as they go about their everyday activities. Flipper bands are placed around a penguin's flipper joint in order to identify individual birds for study. With different combinations of colors and numbers, these bands allow researchers to identify individuals at a distance without having to handle them. Since the 1950s, thou-

A band has been placed around this Adélie penguin's flipper joint. Some researchers fear that such bands interfere with normal penguin activities.

sands of penguins have been banded every year. Data from several studies seem to bear out concerns about banding. In a report of their study examining the affects of flipper bands on king penguins, Guillaume Froget and his colleagues summarize some of the possible problems:

> Some data suggest that the added energy cost due to one flipper band may be as high as 24% for swimming penguins. . . . Another possible effect is an increase in predation due to the flipper bands either acting as a "flasher" for penguins' predators or increasing the vulnerability of penguins through a decrease in locomotory ability. Flipper bands may also have adverse effects on penguins through discomfort or by inducing trauma or wounds. [23]

In their study Froget and his colleagues found that banded penguins began breeding later in the year than unbanded birds. They attribute this delay to the increased effort it took for the banded birds to travel and forage. They speculate that banded penguins would take longer to capture enough food to build up the energy reserves necessary to begin breeding.

Although their study demonstrated that banding can negatively impact penguins, Froget and his colleagues admit that they were not able to estimate the overall implications for penguins' survival. Therefore, they recommend further study into the question as well as the development of alternative techniques for the marking and long-term monitoring of penguins.

Long-term study of Magellanic penguins

Despite the possible negative impacts that some of these research techniques may have on individual penguins, scientists contend that they have gained important insights into the lives and behavior of their study subjects. In one of the most significant long-term studies of penguins to date, University of Washington zoologist Dr. Dee Boersma has utilized a variety of research techniques to develop a comprehensive picture of the biology and behavior of Magellanic penguins. Since 1982 Boersma and her colleagues have studied a breeding colony of penguins in Punta Tombo, Argentina, compiling data on reproduction, behavior, and conservation issues.

In the course of her research, Boersma has banded over fifty thousand penguins and what she has learned is that the Punta Tombo colony has steadily decreased in size over the last ten years. In the breeding season of 2000, thousands of dead penguins washed up on beaches in the region and many birds abandoned their nests. Penguins that remained appeared undernourished and in poor condition. "This is the worst year ever, and we keep getting a lot of bad years,"[24] reported Boersma. Fortunately, the penguins of Punta Tombo had a better year in 2001, returning to their nest sites at higher body weights and breeding more successfully than in many previous years. Despite the good year, Boersma is concerned that human pressures affecting the penguins of Punta Tombo will result in a continued overall decline in numbers.

Studying the effects of El Niño

These fluctuations in breeding success are thought to primarily be a result of changes in food availability from year to year. Fishing activity in the region and the effects of oil pollution may play a role, but Boersma and her colleagues think that one of the most significant influences is a phenomenon called the El Niño/Southern Oscillation event. El Niño is a naturally occurring event that takes place sporadically every few years. During an El Niño, the waters along the west coast of South America and across the equatorial Pacific warm up, causing the fish that penguins prey upon to seek colder waters, which are far from penguin breeding areas. El Niños, scientists believe, can cause significant shortages of prey for Magellanic, Humboldt, and Galápagos penguins.

Boersma has spent considerable time studying the endangered Galápagos penguins and has observed that seasons of low breeding success coincide with El Niño events. Because Galápagos penguins live along the equator, their survival is totally dependent on the cool currents that support the schools of fish they prey upon. During the El Niño event of 1972, for example, Boersma observed almost total nesting failure in Galápagos penguins; all but one of two hundred nests found failed to produce any chicks. Even more severe was the 1982–1983 El Niño, in which lack of food not only caused

The Lure of Penguins

In his book *Waiting to Fly,* Ron Naveen describes the irresistible attraction that he feels toward penguins and their Antarctic environment:

I'm affected on various and sundry levels. Superficially, I'm lured like everyone else: The penguins' upright stance and animated behavior reminds me too much of my own waddling around, sometimes unsteadily. . . . But the infection runs deeper. Consider where chinstraps, gentoos, and Adélies live: Antarctica. It's the one spot on the planet that no human rules, that no ownership possesses—a strange location where people from more than forty countries, representing 75 percent of the world's population, work together harmoniously. Antarctica is the last frontier on the planet—a mix of unspoiled beauty, heart-tugging wildlife, and history, which has been explored only within the last two or three generations, essentially within the time frame of our parents and grandparents. So in my complicated view, chinstraps, gentoos, and Adélies stand before me as research subject, as messenger, and as symbol—and they continually lure me back. They keep me on my toes, keep me thinking, and force me to wonder how it might be, if I—if all of us—had a less dominating view of the planet.

An appealing Adélie penguin takes an unsteady stroll.

breeding failure but also killed large numbers of adult birds. During this time period the population of Galápagos penguins fell by 77 percent. Throughout the 1980s, reproduction was poor and the population made only small gains, although some twenty-five years later seems to be recovering. Boermsa worries, however, that gains made by this recovery could be quickly erased by another El Niño event. She explains why the Galápagos penguins seem to be hardest hit by the effects of El Niño: "Galápagos penguins can not avoid poor food conditions by migrating long distances because outside of the Galápagos there are no suitable foraging areas. . . . By banding birds and observing them I found Galápagos penguins rarely go farther than a few hundred meters from shore and they often remain near their breeding site year round."[25]

Given the precarious numbers among temperate penguin species, scientists are alarmed at what could happen should a severe El Niño return to the Pacific. "If we get a series of intense El Niños, they're going to disappear," explains Dr. Patricia Majluf, a biologist studying Humboldt penguins. "We lost half during one bad El Niño and these are very slow breeding birds."[26]

Studies such as these point to the serious situation facing many penguin species today. However, even as census data show continued decrease in some species' numbers, biologists are concerned that the penguins' problems have gone largely unnoticed. Fortunately, increasing conservation efforts for penguins in both temperate and polar regions are beginning to attract the attention of both scientists and the general public, bringing much needed attention to the penguins' plight.

5

Penguin Conservation

SINCE THE 1970s, direct threats to penguins, such as hunting and egg gathering, have largely been eliminated. Overcoming current threats, such as pollution, overfishing, habitat loss, and introduced predators, is more challenging since these are "more insidious because they're usually widespread, complex, difficult to control, and likely to increase,"[27] according to Dr. Dee Boersma. Fortunately, penguins have a number of allies trying to protect them. Government agencies, conservation organizations, scientists, and zoos are increasingly working together to ease the plight of penguins through research, education, the creation of new laws, and the establishment of protected wildlife areas.

Establishing reserves

In March 1998, the government of Ecuador established one of the world's largest protected areas, the Galápagos Marine Reserve. Encompassing some eighty thousand square miles, the reserve supports a large variety of wildlife found nowhere else in the world, including the Galápagos penguin. This region's designation as a reserve puts in place restrictions on fishing and other activities that may harm the ecosystem—an important step in assuring the future survival of its wildlife.

Another place where wildlife conservation has become a government priority is the Falkland Islands, off the coast of Argentina. The Falklands, a British territory consisting of 778 islands, are home to millions of penguins, including the world's largest concentration of rockhopper penguins (300,000 pairs) and a quarter of the world's gentoo penguins (about 65,000

As if sitting for a portrait, rockhopper penguins strike a pose. The Falkland Islands are home to the world's largest population of rockhoppers.

pairs). In addition, the Falklands serve as an important breeding site for Magellanic penguins (100,000 pairs) and small numbers of king (400 pairs) and macaroni (100 pairs) penguins.

Penguins on the Falklands receive legal protection through measures such as the Conservation of Wildlife and Nature Bill, passed by the Falkland Islands Legislative Council in 1999. This bill prohibits the killing of penguins and other native birds of the Falklands, and also forbids disturbing nesting birds or their eggs. In addition to enacting laws to safeguard wildlife, the Falkland Islands have also established a network of reserves, managed by the government and environmental organizations, that are set aside as protected areas for animals.

The network of reserves in the Falklands was greatly enhanced in March 2002 when Michael Steinhardt, a philanthropist from New York, donated two privately owned, uninhabited islands to the Wildlife Conservation Society (WCS), an American conservation organization working in the region since the 1960s. Called Steeple Jason and Grand Jason, these islands are home to nesting populations of hundreds of thousands of birds, including eighty-nine thousand pairs of rockhopper penguins. The donation of this land also included funds for the development of a research station from which WCS biologists will perform ecosystem studies.

Dr. William Conway, senior conservation biologist for WCS, conducted a survey of the Jason islands and remarked on their dramatic concentrations of wildlife. "The Falkland Islands have some of the last great masses of birds and the Jasons' colonies are particularly spectacular. It's truly awe-inspiring. It is the sort of thing that makes one feel small."[28] In describing the donation of these extraordinary islands, WCS president Dr. Steven Sanderson said, "At a time when wild places supporting great gatherings of animals are fewer and fewer, it is uncommon to be given a landscape of this importance and biological integrity to protect. It is even more uncommon to find the individual who has the vision and understanding to appreciate all that can be learned at such a place."[29]

Regulating fishing to conserve South American penguins

Despite the positive steps that have been taken to conserve the Falkland Islands' wildlife, problems still remain. Census results indicate that penguin populations throughout the Falklands continue to fall. In the 1980s and 1990s gentoo penguins declined by 40 percent; rockhoppers declined by 90 percent from 1940 through 2000. These decreases in penguin numbers are thought to be directly related to changes in their marine environment, such as pollution and overfishing. Research shows that fishing, especially, has played a significant role.

Biologists have studied the impact that decreased food availability, as a result of commercial fishing, has had on penguin foraging and breeding activities. They compared populations of Magellanic penguins on the Falkland Islands, where largely unregulated commercial fishing took place, to those on Chile's Magdalena Island, where fishing activities were prohibited in the penguins' primary feeding areas, a region extending approximately twenty miles from shore. The results of the comparison were striking. Falkland Islands penguins took nearly twice as long (thirty-four hours) to complete foraging trips to feed their chicks as did Magdalena birds (eighteen hours). The Falklands birds had half the breeding success of the Magdalena penguins and their chicks weighed substantially less at fledging. Overall, the Magdalena population was increasing while the Falklands' population was decreasing.

Biologist Dr. Mike Bingham is certain that the poor breeding success of penguins in the Falklands is a result of commercial fishing activities.

> It is impossible to give an accurate total for Magellanic penguins in the Falklands, but we do know that study sites monitored throughout the Falklands during the 1990s have shown a 70% decline over the last 10 years, a decline which is still occurring. It has been suggested that these declines are part of a global trend, but that is not the case. Magellanic and Southern rockhopper penguins are only found in the Falklands and South America, and there are no signs of decline in Chile or Tierra del Fuego. Indeed the closest colonies to the Falklands on Isla Magdalena (Chile) and Staten Island (Argentina) appear to have increased as Falklands populations declined. [30]

Despite their population declines, the Falkland Islands penguin populations now seem to have stabilized. Bingham says, "The good news is that Falklands rockhoppers and gentoos do appear to have reached a new equilibrium that is now in balance with current food availability. Provided that commercial fishing continues to be carefully managed, these

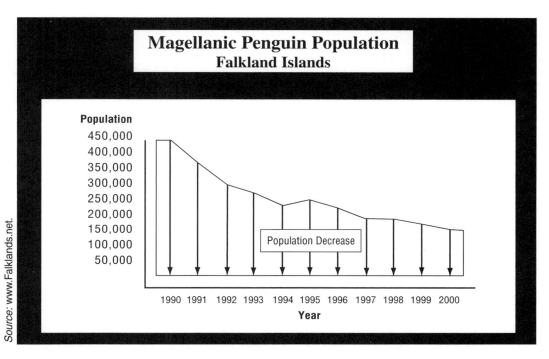

Magellanic Penguin Population
Falkland Islands

Population

450,000
400,000
350,000
300,000
250,000
200,000
150,000
100,000
50,000

Population Decrease

1990 1991 1992 1993 1994 1995 1996 1997 1998 1999 2000
Year

Source: www.Falklands.net.

populations should remain safe, albeit at a lower level than prior to commercial fishing."[31]

The government of the Falkland Islands is beginning to re-examine fishing regulations and determine ways to sustain the marine food supply for both people and wildlife. Finding ways of balancing the needs of both people and wildlife is becoming increasingly important as conservationists struggle to protect animals living near human activity. Biologists now recognize that the concerns of local people must be addressed in order to gain their support for conservation efforts. This strategy, often referred to as community-based conservation, is becoming the preferred approach to protecting wildlife worldwide.

This concept has been applied successfully in Argentina with the development of the Patagonian Coastal Zone Management Plan, beginning in 1993. Developed by several co-operating organizations, including the United Nations Development Programme (UNDP), the Patagonia Nature Foundation, and the Argentine government, this plan addresses the protection of the region's rich wildlife heritage in the face of its rapidly expanding commercial fishery, oil exploration, and growing tourism industry. The objective of the plan was to allow local people opportunities to develop industries such as commercial fishing and wildlife-related tourism while protecting the environment. In practice this meant changing fishing regulations to allow local fishermen access to specific fishing zones that are off limits to commercial fleets from other countries. In exchange for this protection from international competition, these fishermen agreed to avoid fishing in environmentally sensitive areas.

In addition to improving fishing practices, the plan also addressed improving management of nature reserves and employed a public awareness campaign to garner support for marine environment issues. The implementation of the plan has had clear benefits. According to the UNDP, "Communities are now more vocal in demanding protection of the coastal environment and more aware of the need to reduce

Magellanic penguins on the Falkland Islands look out to sea. The Magellanic population there declined steeply during the 1990s.

effluents and the dumping of refuse at sea. . . . [The plan has helped to] provide economic benefits to communities and lessen conflicts between conservation and development." [32]

The Antarctic Treaty

At the same time that many nations are taking steps to protect their own wildlife, some nations are trying to cooperate to preserve habitat lying outside their own borders. For example, nations are attempting to work together to protect the vast wilderness of Antarctica. Since its discovery, portions of Antarctica have been claimed as territory by nine different countries. The governments of these countries have not always agreed upon the future of development in the Antarctic and as the potential value of the marine, mineral, and oil resources of Antarctica were recognized, beginning in the 1940s, rivalry between nations over their territorial claims intensified. As technology improved in the 1950s, scientists were able to gain easier access to the continent and began to establish permanent research bases there, often in an effort to more vigorously assert their nations' territorial claims.

During this time, the Cold War was at its peak, adding another alarming element to the continuing territorial disputes and threatening to disrupt scientific collaboration in the region. In the mid-1950s a group of scientists approached the United Nations with the idea of creating a cooperative, multination research program in Antarctica. The result was the International Geophysical Year (IGY). This "year"—actually eighteen months, from July 1957 through December 1958— was a period in which the twelve nations, all of which had been active in trying to develop the natural resources of Antarctica, worked together in a spirit of scientific discovery. The IGY proved to be a turning point in international politics as they related to the Antarctic. The participating nations agreed that peaceful, scientific cooperation in Antarctica should continue indefinitely, with the goal of providing benefits for people of all nations. The result was the creation of the Antarctic Treaty. Signed on December 1, 1959, by the twelve nations active in the IGY, the treaty contains fourteen articles guaranteeing that "Antarctica shall continue for ever

Antarctic Site Inventory

As a result of the Antarctic Treaty's *Protocol on Environmental Protection,* researchers began an effort in 1994 to compile information about the region. Called the Antarctic Site Inventory, this project will help scientists assess the impact that proposed human activities might have on the environment.

The treaty requires that before any human activities can be conducted, including research and tourism, an assessment must take place to ensure that there will be little or no environmental impact as a result. To understand the impact of an activity, scientists first must have baseline information. The goal of the inventory is to collect that sort of data, such as surveys, censuses, and other environmental monitoring, that will allow scientists to detect any changes. They also hope to use this information to determine how to minimize or avoid potential impacts to the Antarctic.

For example, inventory scientists make repeated visits to areas that are most heavily visited by tourists and therefore the most potentially prone to disturbance by people. They also study the sites at times of the year that are key to the penguin life cycle, such as egg laying or chick fledging. Within these sites, scientists study penguins both close to the visitor landing areas and those farther away that are less frequently disturbed.

Three types of information are gathered by inventory scientists: basic site information, including the locations of penguin breeding sites; variable site information, including numbers of penguin nests and chicks and signs of human impact (for example, trash or paths); and maps documenting the colonies. Over time, this data will allow the researchers to make comparisons between areas of great and little human activity to determine the extent of disruption people cause to the Antarctic ecosystem.

to be used exclusively for peaceful purposes and shall not become the scene or object of international discord."[33] This meant that military action, nuclear testing or radioactive waste disposal, and other nonpeaceful uses of the land and surrounding waters would be prohibited.

Although the treaty was a significant step in protecting the Antarctic environment, concern remained about the impact Antarctic exploration and tourism would have on the penguins and other unique wildlife of the region. To ensure that comprehensive protection was provided to Antarctica, the treaty was amended to include additional agreements such as conservation of the region's plants and animals, management of protected areas, and management of tourism. Collectively these agreements are known as the Antarctic Treaty System (ATS). The ATS is open to any member of the United Nations; currently forty-four countries have signed the treaty.

The ATS is open to expansion through additional agreements. One of the most recent additions to the ATS is the Protocol on Environmental Protection, ratified by all member nations in 1997. The protocol established environmental principles to govern all activities in Antarctica. This means that any proposed project must be evaluated for its potential

A tourist extends a friendly hand to a king penguin. The Antarctic Treaty calls for management both of tourism and of protected areas on the continent.

impact on the environment. The protocol also bans mining on the continent for a minimum of fifty years and updates rules for conserving the region's plants and animals, including provisions for conducting animal research. For example, to minimize disturbance, vehicles and helicopters are forbidden to go near penguin colonies. In addition, the protocol provides for the management and disposal of waste generated by research stations and the prevention of marine pollution. This agreement is a major victory for Antarctic conservation, says Beth Clark, director of the Antarctica Project: "By establishing high standards for all human activities in the region, the Environmental Protocol goes a long way towards safeguarding Antarctica before it suffers from the human impacts felt over most of the rest of the earth."[34]

Penguin Conservation Assessment and Management Plan

Even as national governments work together to preserve the Antarctic and the wildlife living there, biologists are banding together to safeguard penguins, sharing information gained through their respective research efforts in order to develop a comprehensive understanding of the status of penguins worldwide. To that end, thirty-seven people from ten countries gathered in Cape Town, South Africa, in 1996 to participate in a penguin Conservation Assessment and Management Plan (CAMP) workshop. Participants, including zoo biologists, field biologists, and academics, focused on compiling all available information on penguin species in order to determine conservation priorities. The result was a strategy guiding penguin conservation by outlining further research needs, conservation action steps, and a plan for captive breeding.

Participants came away from the workshop with a renewed sense of urgency regarding efforts to protect penguins. The summary of the CAMP workshop describes a picture of the perilous status of penguins:

> The results of the workshop were startling and alarming. Of all the penguin species, only those in the Antarctic do not seem to be facing grave, documented declines or other problems that put

them at serious risk. Even Antarctic species are not secure in perpetuity—the threats that have put the other penguin species at risk also have the potential to affect Antarctic species. . . . It also is disturbing that some of the more globally abundant species (Rockhopper, Macaroni and Magellanic Penguins) have declined in abundance over the last three generations, and qualify for Vulnerable and Near Threatened status.[35]

Adélie penguins dive into the sea in Antarctica. Researchers say that the Antarctic species are the only penguins not facing serious problems.

The CAMP summary emphasizes that the future of penguins is dependent on the health of their marine environment and that threats such as competition from commercial fisheries and ocean pollution may lead to further population declines or even the extinction of some penguin species. Therefore, CAMP workshop participants recommended further research as a penguin conservation priority. To better understand the penguin's place in marine ecology, they encourage further investigation into penguins' foraging behavior, the extent of their conflicts with fisheries, and how they are affected by pollution.

Penguins at SeaWorld Parks

The SeaWorld Parks in Orlando, Florida, San Diego, California, and San Antonio, Texas, are home to North America's most elaborate penguin exhibits. Between the three parks, SeaWorld animal care staff manage between eight hundred and nine hundred individual birds representing nine species: emperor, king, gentoo, chinstrap, Adélie, macaroni, rockhopper, Magellanic, and Humboldt. The penguin exhibits are specially designed to simulate the terrain, temperature, and light cycles that the species would naturally encounter in their Southern Hemisphere habitats. This careful attention to the special needs of captive penguins has paid off; breeding has been very successful at the parks. A member of the education department staff, in personal communication with the author, explains the management of penguin breeding at one SeaWorld facility:

> In Florida we install the rookery or nesting area in mid-September (the austral spring for the penguins). The birds immediately start building nests with the smooth river rocks that we provide the smaller species. Within two weeks, the first eggs are laid, as pairs often return to the same mates and nest sites annually. We prefer to leave the eggs and chicks with the parents, however, we will artificially incubate and hand rear a chick, if necessary. If a pair has a history of poor parenting or improper incubation, we might foster their egg to another pair who may have had an infertile egg, or place the egg in the incubator if suitable foster parents are not available. The king and emperor penguins do not build a nest like the smaller species do; they incubate their single egg on top of their feet. We do remove the parent-reared chicks from their parents at three weeks of age in Orlando, so they may safely fledge and become accustomed to feeding from the aviculturists. We then return them to the exhibit once they are fledged and waterproofed, where they are closely observed for safe exiting from the pool.

Penguins in zoos

In addition to determining the research and conservation needs of penguins in the wild, the penguin CAMP also examined areas in which zoo biologists could collaborate with field biologists, forming partnerships to provide strong benefits for penguins. Because their numbers are not yet extremely low, most penguin species are not in need of captive breeding programs for conservation purposes. The CAMP recognized, however, that the keeping of penguins in zoos and aquariums plays an important research and education role. For example, zoo penguins may be used to test new flipper band designs in an effort to improve their value in research and minimize potential harm to the birds. Captive penguins may also serve as models in research of penguin diseases that impact wild populations. Because zoo-based penguin biologists themselves are an important resource for work with wild penguins, CAMP recommended the development of a penguin oil response team consisting of zoo staff that will provide experienced penguin handlers to assist in treating penguins following a major oil spill.

The penguin CAMP also recognized that one of the most important roles for penguins in zoos and aquariums is that of goodwill ambassadors for their species as well as representatives of their imperiled marine environment. The eleven

Aside from being useful research subjects, penguins living in zoos serve as walking advertisements for the need to preserve their species.

species of penguins housed and displayed in North American zoos are among those facilities' most popular exhibits, providing opportunities for extensive public education to take place. Because few people have the opportunity to observe penguins in the wild, zoos are important for fostering awareness and teaching visitors about these engaging birds. In fact, education is an important goal of the American Zoo and Aquarium Association's Penguin Taxon Advisory Group (TAG). The Penguin TAG, a group of experts in caring for captive penguins, provides leadership in the management of penguins in zoos throughout North America in order to maintain healthy populations and develop penguin conservation initiatives.

The Penguin TAG works with zoos toward the goals of promoting an appreciation of penguins by zoo visitors, encouraging visitors to take conservation action, and furthering research in support of both captive management and conservation of penguins in the wild. In their efforts to best manage captive penguins, members of the Penguin TAG evaluate which species of penguin zoos should exhibit, how many individuals of each species should be housed, and which individuals should be bred. Because there is a limited amount of space for housing penguins in zoos, certain species may take priority. TAG members evaluating the value of exhibiting a particular species examine a number of criteria, including the species' potential to impact conservation; its scientific or research value; its status in the wild; the health of the captive population; and the existence of a captive population.

The Penguin TAG manages most captive penguin species through one of two strategies. One strategy is a species survival plan (SSP). A species covered by an SSP is intensively managed through the use of a studbook that records the ancestry and breeding history of all the individuals of the population. This studbook is consulted to determine which animals should be paired for breeding in order to assure the long-term genetic health of the population. Two penguin species, the Humboldt and African, are managed through SSPs. The remaining captive species are managed through a population management plan (PMP). A PMP also uses a studbook to record the breeding history of the individuals,

"What Good Are Penguins?"

George Gaylord Simpson, one of the world's leading penguin biologists, summarized his feelings about the value of penguins in his classic work *Penguins Past and Present, Here and There,* published in 1976.

Finally the question may be asked, "What good are penguins?" It may be crass to ask what good a wild animal is, but I do think the question may also be legitimate. That depends on what you mean by good. If you mean "good to eat," you are perhaps being stupid. If you mean "good to hunt," you are surely being vicious. If you mean "good as it is good in itself to be a living creature enjoying life," you are not being crass, stupid, or vicious. I agree with you and I am your brother as well as the penguin's.

Penguins are valuable members of nature's community. Here, a bevy of emperor chicks huddles for warmth.

but the population is not as intensively managed, generally because PMP populations are more secure.

Although a variety of education and conservation initiatives are now being undertaken on behalf of penguins, such as captive breeding, the establishment of parks and reserves, and the creation of laws, many biologists are concerned that these measures do not go nearly far enough to ensure a future for penguins. They point to changes in the global environment as further challenges for an already embattled marine ecosystem. Conservationists worry that these emerging threats, such as climate change and greenhouse gas emissions, may be another hazard pushing penguins ever closer to extinction.

Epilogue

DESPITE THE COMBINED efforts of zoos, conservation organizations, and scientists working in the field, the foreseeable future holds little promise that the challenges facing penguins and their marine environment will abate. Many scientists feel that it is time to sound the alarm and raise concerns over the plight of penguins before populations dip so low that recovery would be extremely difficult.

Scientists speculate that, in addition to the threats known to impact penguins, several more may prove to have serious consequences as well. One potential threat is the commercial harvesting of krill that is now increasingly taking place as ocean fish populations are becoming depleted and the fishing industry looks to develop alternate fishery sources. Because krill forms an important link in the food chain for penguins and other Antarctic wildlife, scientists worry about the impact an intensive krill fishery may have on the krill's natural predators—penguins, fish, and seals. The amount of krill that can be harvested sustainably, or not significantly impacting the total population, is a matter of great debate. One estimate is that 1.5 million tons of krill can be taken annually without causing a lack of food for predators. Currently, about 350,000 to 400,000 tons of krill are harvested annually. Although this take may be small compared to the estimate of sustainable take, it may still have a pronounced effect on penguins because fishing activities often take place near penguin nesting colonies. Current laws allow fishing to continue until there is evidence that the take is harmful to the environment. This approach concerns the Antarctic and

The commercial harvest of krill (pictured) is a potential threat to the well-being of penguins and other marine life.

Southern Ocean Coalition (ASOC), an organization committed to environmental conservation in the region. Because of krill's prominent place in the ecosystem, ASOC advocates limiting the krill fishery to low levels until scientists can accurately assess the krill population and better understand predators' needs. ASOC is concerned that by the time proof is available of the damage caused by overfishing of krill, such as the crash of penguin populations, the damage may be irreversible.

Scientists studying the dietary needs of penguins are increasingly backing this viewpoint. Researchers studying king penguins at Heard Island and others studying Adélie, chinstrap, and gentoo penguins in the South Shetland Islands concluded that there is evidence to suggest that krill fisheries compete with penguins. In a report of their findings in the South Shetlands, authors D.A. Croll and B.R. Tershy conclude, "To the extent that penguins and fur seals are food limited, and krill availability is limited by the commercial fishery, populations of these predators will be affected. It is logical, therefore, that they be considered important components of the marine ecosystem when considering fisheries management strategies."[36]

Thinning of the ozone layer

While the overfishing of krill might ultimately have a direct effect on penguins, another phenomenon of concern to penguin biologists is significantly subtler. Since 1977, scientists have been aware of decreasing levels of ozone in the atmosphere above Antarctica. Ozone is an isotope of oxygen that shields the planet from the sun's ultraviolet light. Without sufficient ozone, enough ultraviolet radiation can reach Earth to cause harm to both people and animals. This decrease in the ozone layer is now known to be the result of chemicals called chlorofluorocarbons, or CFCs. CFCs are used in refrigerators, air conditioners, cleaning fluids, and some aerosol products. Significant quantities of CFCs are released into the air, where they react with the ozone, forming compounds that lack the ability to block ultraviolet radiation.

Researchers already know that the Antarctic is the site of a large gap in the atmosphere's ozone layer and they have found that increased ultraviolet radiation reaching Earth during the spring kills plankton, which krill rely on for food. As a result, the amount of krill available as food for penguins also decreases. The collapse of krill stocks, researchers fear, could force penguin parents to forage much further to find enough food for their young. These fears may in fact have already come to pass. In 1995, Australian scientists reported observing penguins searching for food for their chicks as far as 120 miles from shore. Elsewhere in Antarctica during that breeding season, large numbers of penguin chicks were found to have starved to death. Although the cause of their food shortage was unknown, some scientists theorize that the thinning ozone may have played a key role.

Climate change

In addition to concerns about the effects ozone depletion may have on Antarctic penguins, scientists are increasingly finding evidence that Earth's changing climate may also jeopardize the birds' future. Global warming, or the increase in Earth's average temperature, has become an area of intense study worldwide. Scientists say that global warming is the result of increasing amounts of carbon dioxide and other gases released as a byproduct of burning fossil fuels such as coal, gasoline, and diesel. These gases accumulate in the atmosphere, where they trap heat that would otherwise be released into space, a process known as the "greenhouse effect." Researchers widely agree that as the production and release of greenhouse gases grows with human activity, more and more heat will be trapped, causing temperatures to gradually rise.

The greatest increases in temperature on the planet are being recorded on the Antarctic Peninsula, a seven-hundred-mile stretch of land jutting from the continent. Over the twentieth century, as human industry has intensified, temperatures have increased worldwide by 1 degree Fahrenheit. Yet, on the Antarctic Peninsula, the temperature has jumped more than 5 degrees in only fifty years. Dr. William Fraser, a scientist at Palmer Station research base who has been studying the region's climate since 1974, observes, "When I was a graduate student, we were told that climate change occurs but we'd never see the effects in our lifetime. But in the last 20 years I've seen tremendous changes. I've seen islands pop out from under glaciers; I've seen species changing places and landscape ecology altered."[37] Fraser and other researchers speculate that the changing Antarctic climate is taking its toll on penguins in two ways: by leading to a decreased food supply and by causing declining nesting success. In other words, penguins are subject to changes of both their marine and terrestrial habitats.

When temperatures rise in Antarctica, ice begins to melt; the amount of sea ice surrounding the Antarctic Peninsula has been declining gradually since the 1970s. Krill feed in part on the algae that grow on the bottom of sea ice, so as this ice disappears, so do the krill that constitute the penguins' food supply. Fraser has observed among Adélies between 1975 and 1992, a drop from 15,200 breeding pairs to 9,200 pairs. In this same period, twenty-one Adélie colonies from five islands in the area disappeared altogether.

Fraser and his colleagues speculate that these shrinking and disappearing colonies are due in part to a declining food supply. Additionally, however, they have recently discovered that breeding colonies are also impacted by the increased snowfall brought about by the region's higher temperatures. Warmer temperatures increase the moisture held in the atmosphere, leading to heavier snowfall, which can negatively affect breeding penguins. When penguins are forced to lay their eggs on snow instead of rocks or ice, their nests become wet and slushy as their body heat melts the snow. Penguins

Scientists on snowmobiles leave their research station in Antarctica to travel to a penguin colony.

These Adélie chicks were born on rocks. Penguin chicks born on snow may die when their nests become wet and slushy.

are well adapted to handle extreme cold, but this wet environment often results in the death of chicks and eggs that become chilled.

Fraser's findings are explained in the journal *Science:*

> But "just as we were beginning to feel pretty smug" that sea ice changes accounted for the trends, Fraser says, he and his colleagues noticed an odd geographical pattern to Adelie rookeries. On Litchfield Island, where the number of breeding pairs dropped 43% between 1975 and 1992, the thriving nesting colonies were concentrated on the island's northeast side. The abandoned rookeries, by contrast, were on the southwest side of the island's rocky middle ridge, where more snow accumulates as storms sweep over the islands. . . . "If you're not breeding in the right place, you're in trouble" Fraser says. . . . He thinks that retreating sea ice probably is the main driving force behind the drop in Adelie populations, but "superimposed on that" he says may be the effects of more snowfall in early spring when the birds begin breeding.[38]

Perhaps through the insights provided by scientific studies such as Fraser's, people will be able to recognize the early warnings of potential disaster for penguins and therefore be involved in affecting change. Environmentalist William Ashworth agrees. "We need not watch helplessly as they waddle toward Armageddon. We can intervene. And the cold, rich waters of the southern and northern seas can continue to throng with the graceful flights of these birds that swim with their wings, treating the deep green space of the water like the blue space of the air."[39]

Notes

Introduction

1. Quoted in Remy Marion, *Penguins: A Worldwide Guide.* New York: Sterling, 1995, p. 118.

Chapter 1: Meet the Penguins

2. Art Wolfe and William Ashworth, *Penguins, Puffins, and Auks: Their Lives and Behavior.* New York: Crown, 1993, pp. 22–27.

3. Cherry Kearton, *The Island of Penguins.* New York: Robert M. McBride, 1931, pp. 240–41.

4. Fred Bruemmer, "Birds with an Attitude," *International Wildlife,* May/June 1998, p. 44.

5. Roger Tory Peterson, *Penguins.* Boston: Houghton Mifflin, 1979, p. 125.

6. James Gorman, *The Total Penguin.* New York: Prentice-Hall, 1990, p. 62.

7. Gorman, *The Total Penguin,* p. 65.

Chapter 2: Threats to Penguins

8. Quoted in Gorman, *The Total Penguin,* p. 176.

9. Marion, *Penguins,* p. 121.

10. Marion, *Penguins,* p. 121.

11. Quoted in Gorman, *The Total Penguin,* p. 94.

12. Quoted in Christine McGourty, "Concern over Antarctic Cruise Ships," *BBC News,* January 4, 2002. http://news.bbc.co.uk.

13. Quoted in Tim Radford, "Terror from Tourists," *Guardian Unlimited,* May 18, 2000. www.guardian.co.uk.

14. Quoted in Radford, "Terror from Tourists."

15. Antarctic and Southern Ocean Coalition, *Antarctic Tourism Information Paper,* July 2001, p. 5. www.asoc.org.

16. Quoted in Radford, "Terror from Tourists."

Chapter 3: Ocean Pollution

17. Liguang Sun and Zhonqing Xie, "Changes in Lead Concentration in Antarctic Penguin Droppings During the Past 3,000 Years," *Environmental Geology,* 40, 2001, p. 1,207.

18. Quoted in Les Line, "Into the Abyss?" National Wildlife Federation, 1997. www.nwf.org.

19. Quoted in CNN.com, "Rescuers Help Threatened Birds After Oil Spill off South African Coast," June 30, 2000. www.cnn.com.

Chapter 4: Studying Penguins

20. Yolanda van Heezik and Philip Seddon, "Penguins Under the Sun," *Natural History,* November 1997.

21. Van Heezik and Seddon, "Penguins Under the Sun."

22. Ron Naveen, *Waiting to Fly: My Escapades with the Penguins of Antartica.* New York: William Morrow, 1999, pp. 67–68.

23. Guillaume Froget, Michel Gautier-Clerc, Yvon Le Maho, and Yves Handrich, "Is Penguin Banding Harmless?" *Polar Biology* (20), 1998, p. 409.

24. Quoted in Carol Kaesuk Yoon, "Penguins in Trouble Worldwide," *New York Times,* June 26, 2001, p. F1.

25. P. Dee Boersma, "Impacts of El Niño on Galápagos Penguins' Body Condition and Movement," *Proceedings of the American Association for the Advancement of Science, Pacific Division* 18 (1), 1999, p. 43.

26. Quoted in Yoon, "Penguins in Trouble Worldwide," p. F1.

Chapter 5: Penguin Conservation

27. Quoted in Les Line, "Into the Abyss?"

28. Quoted in *Wildlife Conservation Society News,* "Spectacular Falkland Islands with Vast Penguin and Albatross Colonies Given to WCS," March 5, 2002. http://wcs.org.

29. Quoted in *Wildlife Conservation Society News,* "Spectacular Falkland Islands."

30. Mike Bingham, "The Ups and Downs of Falklands Penguins," *Conservation Online.* www.conservationonline.com.

31. Bingham, "The Ups and Downs of Falklands Penguins," *Conservation Online.*

32. United Nations Development Programme, "Patagonian Coastal Zone Management Plan." www.undp.org.

33. Quoted in Antarctic and Southern Ocean Coalition, "The Antarctic Treaty System." www.asoc.org.

34. Quoted in Greenpeace Antarctica Press Release, "Historic Antarctic Protection Agreement Becomes Law," December 16, 1997. archive.greenpeace.org.

35. *Penguin Conservation Assessment and Management Plan,* IUCN Conservation Breeding Specialist Group, 1996, pp. ii, iii, iv. www.cbsg.org.

Epilogue

36. D.A. Croll and B.R. Tershy, "Penguins, Fur Seals, and Fishing: Prey Requirements and Potential Competition in the South Shetland Islands, Antarctica." *Polar Biology (19),* 1998, p. 372.

37. Quoted in David Helvarg, "Fiddling While Antarctica Burns," *New York Times,* March 7, 1999, p.15.

38. Jocelyn Kaiser, "Is Warming Trend Harming Penguins?" *Science,* June 20, 1997, p. 1,790.

39. Wolfe and Ashworth, *Penguins, Puffins, and Auks,* p. 198.

Glossary

census: A scientifically accurate counting of the number of individual animals in a given area.

colony: A distinct grouping of nesting penguins; groups of colonies make up a rookery.

countershading: The black-and-white coloration pattern on a penguin's body that provides camouflage while it swims.

endangered species: An animal or plant that has been scientifically determined to be at risk of extinction in all or a significant part of its range within the foreseeable future.

extinction: The disappearance of a species of plant or animal.

guano: Penguin droppings.

habitat: An area that provides the physical elements needed by a certain animal or plant species.

incubation: The process of keeping an egg warm prior to hatching.

krill: Shrimplike crustaceans that form the basis of the Antarctic food chain, providing a large part of the diet for many penguin species.

pelagic: Describing an animal that spends most of its time at sea, away from land.

porpoising: A penguin swimming style during which penguins periodically leap into the air to breathe.

population: The total number of individuals within a given area.

preen: The act of a bird distributing oil from a gland at the base of its tail in order to align and waterproof its feathers.

rookery: Traditional breeding grounds used by penguins over many generations, often numbering in the hundreds of thousands of individual birds.

species: A category of biological classification denoting a group of physically similar organisms that breed with each other.

Spheniscidae: The scientific name for the penguin family.

SSP: Species Survival Plan. A plan drawn up by the American Zoo and Aquarium Association to help ensure the future of selected species through tightly controlled captive breeding practices.

thermoregulation: Maintaining a constant body temperature through biological or behavioral means.

Organizations to Contact

The Antarctica Project
1630 Connecticut Ave. NW,
3rd Floor
Washington, D.C. 20009
(202) 234-2480
www.asoc.org

The only conservation organization devoted exclusively to the Antarctic, the Antarctica Project provides information on a wide variety of the region's environmental issues including the Antarctic Treaty and tourism. Visit their website to learn action steps to take to help protect the Antarctic environment.

The Charles Darwin Research Station
Puerto Ayora, Isla Santa Cruz
Galápagos Islands, Ecuador
www.darwinfoundation.org

The Charles Darwin Research Station conducts scientific research to assist the Galápagos National Park Service and also conducts environmental education programs for the local community, schools, and visitors to the islands. Major research programs include the monitoring of wildlife populations, the eradication of introduced pest species, and natural resource management.

Falklands Conservation
1 Princes Ave.
Finchley, London
N3 2DA United Kingdom
www.falklandsconservation.com

This conservation organization monitors and protects the unique wildlife heritage of the Falkland Islands. Their website provides information on penguins, access to conservation newsletters, and adopt-a-penguin opportunities.

South African National Foundation for the Conservation of Coastal Birds (SANCCOB)
P.O. Box 11116
Bloubergrant, Cape Town, 7443
www.sanccob.co.za

SANCCOB has successfully rehabilitated and released over eighty thousand injured and oiled seabirds since it was established in 1968. Visit their website for stories about penguin rescues and to learn how to help by making a donation or adopting a penguin.

For Further Reading

Books

Rebecca L. Johnson, *Science on the Ice*. Minneapolis: Lerner, 1995. The author documents her journey to Antarctica where she joined scientists as they conducted their research studying the wildlife, geology, and atmosphere of the frozen continent.

Remy Marion, *Penguins: A Worldwide Guide*. New York: Sterling, 1995. A concise overview of the natural history of the penguin species as well as a chronicle of humans' impact on them.

Ron Naveen, *Waiting to Fly: My Escapades with the Penguins of Antarctica*. New York: William Morrow, 1999. A scientist with sixteen years of experience studying penguins relates many of his most memorable encounters.

Art Wolfe and William Ashworth, *Penguins, Puffins, and Auks: Their Lives and Behavior*. New York: Crown, 1993. A comprehensive account of the biology, behavior, and conservation issues of penguins fully illustrated with remarkable photos by famed wildlife photographer Art Wolfe.

Websites

International Penguin Conservation Working Group (www.penguins.cl). Visit this site to learn about the threats facing penguins and research currently underway. Excellent species accounts provide links to specific organizations working with rare penguins.

Penguin Studies Page (http://faculty.washington.edu/boersma). This site provides news and updates of the research of Dr. P. Dee

Boersma and her team. Dr. Boersma provides answers to frequently asked questions about penguin studies in audio and Quick Time video.

Penguin Taxon Advisory Group (www.penguintag.org). This site provides descriptions of each penguin species as well as links to the websites of zoos exhibiting them. Also included is a penguin bibliography.

Works Consulted

Books

Lloyd S. Davis and John T. Darby, eds., *Penguin Biology.* San Diego: Academic Press, 1990. A comprehensive academic volume detailing the current and historic scientific study of penguins.

James Gorman, *The Total Penguin.* New York: Prentice-Hall, 1990. An entertaining account of the history and lives of penguins.

Cherry Kearton, *The Island of Penguins.* New York: Robert M. McBride, 1931. A historic account of a naturalist's observations of African penguins.

Roger Tory Peterson, *Penguins.* Boston: Houghton Mifflin, 1979. This work by a famed naturalist examines the lives of penguins and their history with humans, with particular focus on threats to penguins.

Diana Preston, *A First Rate Tragedy: Robert Falcon Scott and the Race to the South Pole.* New York: Houghton Mifflin, 1998. An account of the historic exploration of the South Pole.

Pauline Reilly, *Penguins of the World.* Oxford: Oxford University Press, 1994. A guide to the species of penguins including information on description, distribution, feeding, breeding, and conservation needs.

George Gaylord Simpson, *Penguins Past and Present, Here and There.* New Haven: Yale University Press, 1976. A classic volume detailing the penguin's fossil record, descriptions of species, and the history of their relations with humans.

Periodicals

Antarctic and Southern Ocean Coalition, *Antarctic Tourism Information Paper.* July 2001. www.asoc.org.

Antarctic and Southern Ocean Coalition, *Fisheries Fact Sheet.* www.asoc.org.

Antarctic and Southern Ocean Coalition, "The *Antarctic Treaty System."* www.asoc.org.

Grant Ballard, David G. Ainley, Christine A. Ribic, and Kerry R. Barton, "Effect of Instrument Attachment and Other Factors of Foraging Trip Duration and Nesting Success of Adélie Penguins," *Condor,* August 2001.

————, "Galápagos Oil Spill—A Preliminary Overview of the Impacts on the Ecosystem," Charles Darwin Foundation. www.darwinfoundation.org.

Robert Bensted-Smith, "Now It's Time for Clean-Up, Evaluation of Impacts and Monitoring—and to Think About the Future," Charles Darwin Foundation. www.darwinfoundation.org.

Mike Bingham, "The Ups and Downs of Falklands Penguins," *Conservation Online.* www.conservationonline.com.

P. Dee Boersma, "Impacts of El Niño on Galápagos Penguins Body Condition and Movement," *Proceedings of the American Association for the Advancement of Science, Pacific Division* 18 (1), 1999 p. 43.

————, "Population Trends of the Galápagos Penguin: Impacts of El Niño and La Niña," *Condor,* May 1998.

Fred Bruemmer, "Birds with an Attitude," *International Wildlife,* May/June 1998.

Charles Darwin Foundation, "The 'Jessica' Oil Spill: A Year Later." www.darwinfoundation.org.

CNN.com, "Rescuers Help Threatened Birds After Oil Spill off South African Coast," June 30, 2000. www.cnn.com.

Gordon S. Court, "The Seal's Own Skin Game," *Natural History,* August 1996.

D.A. Croll and B.R. Tershy, "Penguins, Fur Seals, and Fishing: Prey Requirements and Potential Competition in the South Shetland Islands, Antarctica." *Polar Biology* (19), 1998.

B.M. Culik and G. Luna-Jorquera, "Satellite Tracking of Humboldt Penguins (*Spheniscus humboldti*) in Northern Chile," *Marine Biology* (128), 1997.

Edward Diebold and Susie Ellis, "Strides in AZA TAG Communication with Field Biologists: The CBSG Penguin CAMP Workshop," *Annual Conference Proceedings of the American Zoo and Aquarium Association,* 1997.

Susie Ellis and Sherry Branch, eds., *Penguin Husbandry Manual.* American Zoo and Aquarium Association, 1994.

Mike Ford, "First Impressions of a SANCCOB Volunteer," Avian Demography Unit, University of Cape Town. www.uct.ac.za.

Guillaume Froget, Michel Gautier-Clerc, Yvon Le Maho, and Yves Handrich, "Is Penguin Banding Harmless?" *Polar Biology* (20), 1998.

Greenpeace Antarctica Press Release, "Historic Antarctic Protection Agreement Becomes Law," December 16, 1997. archive.greenpeace.org.

David Helvarg, "Fiddling While Antarctica Burns," *New York Times,* March 7, 1999.

International Penguin Conservation Work Group, "The Penguins National Nature Reserve: Magdalena Island, Punta Arenas, Chile." www.seabirds.org.

Jocelyn Kaiser, "Is Warming Trend Harming Penguins?" *Science,* June 20, 1997, p. 1,790.

Les Line, "Into the Abyss?" *International Wildlife,* September/ October 1997.

Cathy Lundmark, "Perils for Penguins," *Bioscience,* February 2002.

Hillary Mayell, "Patagonia Penguins Make a Comeback," *National Geographic News,* December 26, 2001. http://news. nationalgeographic.com.

Christine McGourty, "Concern over Antarctic Cruise Ships," *BBC News,* January 4, 2002. http://news.bbc.co.uk.

Geoffrey J. Moore, Graham Robertson, and Barbara Wienecke, "Food Requirements of Breeding King Penguins at Heard Island and Potential Overlap with Commercial Fisheries," *Polar Biology (20),* 1998.

National Science Foundation, "Antarctic Remediation Underway," February 23, 2001.

New York Times, "Spill from Oil Tanker Imperils Rare Wildlife in the Galápagos," January 22, 2001.

Olof Olsson, "The Sea Side of King Penguins," *Natural History,* February 1997.

Penguin Conservation Assessment and Management Plan, IUCN Conservation Breeding Specialist Group, 1996. www.cbsg.org.

Penguin Taxon Advisory Group, Regional Collection Plan 1999–2000.

Tim Radford, "Terror from Tourists," *Guardian Unlimited,* May 18, 2000. www.guardian.co.uk.

———, "Antarctic Penguins Feel the Heat," *Guardian Unlimited,* May 10, 2001. www.guardian.co.uk.

Jana Regel and Klemens Pütz, "Effect of Human Disturbance on Body Temperature and Energy Expenditure in Penguins," *Polar Biology (*18), 1997.

Andrew C. Revkin, "A New Sanctuary Where Penguins No Longer Fear to Tread," *New York Times,* March 5, 2002.

John Roach, "Penguin Decline in Antarctica Linked with Climate Change," *National Geographic News,* May 9, 2001. http://news.nationalgeographic.com.

David L. Stokes, P. Dee Boersma, Lloyd S. Davis, "Satellite Tracking of Magellanic Penguin Migration," *Condor,* May 1998.

Liguang Sun and Zhonqing Xie, "Changes in Lead Concentration in Antarctic Penguin Droppings During the Past 3,000 Years," *Environmental Geology,* (40), 2001.

Les Underhill, "A Brief History of Penguin Oiling in South African Waters," Avian Demography Unit, University of Cape Town. www.uct.ac.za.

United Nations Development Programme, "Patagonian Coastal Zone Management Plan." www.undp.org.

Yolanda van Heezik and Philip Seddon, "Penguins Under the Sun," *Natural History,* November 1997.

P.A. Whittington, "The Contribution Made by Cleaning Oiled African Penguins *Spheniscus demersus* to Population Dynamics and Conservation of the Species," Avian Demography Unit, University of Cape Town. www.uct.ac.za.

Phil Whittington, "The Cape Town Harbour Oil Spill—One Year After the Event," Avian Demography Unit, University of Cape Town. www.uct.ac.za.

Wildlife Conservation Society News, "Spectacular Falkland Islands with Vast Penguin and Albatross Colonies Given to WCS," March 5, 2002. http://wcs.org.

World Wildlife Fund, "Oil Spill 2001." www.worldwildlife.org.

Carol Kaesuk Yoon, "Penguins in Trouble Worldwide," *New York Times,* June 26, 2001.

Howard Youth, "Penguins on Thin Ice," *Zoogoer,* January/February 2000.

Index

Picture Credits

About the Author

Karen Povey received her bachelor's degree in zoology at the University of California, Davis, and her master's degree in education at the University of Washington. She has spent her career as a conservation educator, working to instill in people of all ages an appreciation for wildlife. Karen makes her home in Washington where she manages and presents live animal education programs at Tacoma's Point Defiance Zoo & Aquarium. Karen enjoys traveling with her husband and recently visited the Galápagos Islands where she had the great fortune of snorkeling among a feeding group of endangered Galápagos penguins.